To my fellow literary creators,

Welcome to the enchanting realm of storytelling, where the power of imagination knows no bounds and the pen (or keyboard) is your magic wand.

You may think that writing a full length novel is impossible, but with dedication, you can find your groove. Don't worry about pacing, as a book written in five months may be just as good as a book written in five years.

I was frustrated with different how-to books that pertained to novel writing. One would be about action, one about publishing, and another about developing characters. A lot of these books were bland and boring without graphics. Some of the books were repeating the same ideas, as if they had to hit a certain word count, but most of all, they didn't have ALL the information about novel writing that I was desperately searching for.

Think of this book as a reference book; something you can hold on to when the writing path gets tough. From preparation to publishing, I hope this book can aid in uncomfortable situations, development of ideas, and the dreaded writers block.

For beginner writers, you don't just start on a blank page; it's a canvas waiting to be adorned with the vivid hues of your creativity, whether it be an idea that you've had for quite some time or whether you're just winging it.

You, the author, are the composer of creative words, the alchemist of beautiful sentences, the wizard of immersive plots, and the video game creator of vivid settings.

Welcome to the grand adventure of novel writing, where every sentence is a step closer to a world only you can create.

Thireena Yuki

Alerian Academy

Table of Contents

NOVEL BASICS

Types of Books	1
Themes and Ideas	4
Audience	5
Plot Outline	6
Monomyth	7
The Hero's Journey	11
Character-Driven Journey	12
Character Driven	13
Characters	14
Antagonist and Protagonist	15
The Anti-Hero	16
Anti-Hero Types	17
Common Character Types	18
Jungian Archetypes	19
Character Layout Questions	20
Setting	21

EXPANSION — 23

Action and Adventure	25
Mystery	27
Graphic Novels	29
Literary Fiction	31
Romance	32
Horror	33
Suspense and Thriller	34
Biography and Memoir	35
Poetry	36
Short Stories	37
True Crime	38
Science Fiction	39
Historical Setting	40
Setting Location List	41
Fantasy	43
Fantasy Sub-Genres	44
Primary World	45
Secondary World	46
Portal Fantasy	47
Anthropomorphic Fantasy	48
Paranormal Fantasy	49
Historical Fantasy	50
Mythological Fantasy	51
Science Fantasy	52
Magical Realism	53
Worldbuilding	54

CHARACTERS — 59

Character Appearance	61
Tone and Color	62
Complexion and Skin	63
Eyes and Expression	64
Describing Figures	65
Honing Descriptions	66

Examples of Descriptions 67

Show, Don't Tell 69

MBTI 70

Characteristics 71

Character Flaws 72

Lists of Character Flaws 73

Seven Deadly Sins 75

Character Positives 76

Introverted and Extroverted 77

Emotions 78

Plutchik's Wheel 79

Character Expansion 80

Deviant Behavior 81

Self and Ego 82

Plotlines 83

POV 85

EDITING 87

Grammar Rules? 89

Punctuation 90

Capitalization 91

Compound Sentences 93

Complex Sentences 94

They Said "What?" 95

Tags 97

Paragraphs 98

Spell Check 99

English Vs English 100

Word Choice 101

Using the Thesaurus 102

Creative Wording 103

Situation to Action 105

The Five Senses 106

Sight 107

Touch 109

Taste 111

Sounds 113

Scents 115

Other Senses 116

Conflict 117

Magic Creation 118

Writers Block 119

Polishing the Plot 121

What Authors Say 122

PUBLISHING 123

Pen Names 125

Publish-ready 127

Publishing Company 128

Literary Agent 129

Self-Publishing 131

Getting it Out 133

Money 134

Book Facts 135

Overcome Obstacles 136

What Authors Say 137

Types of Books

ACTION AND ADVENTURE

Action and adventure books constantly have you on the edge of your seat with excitement. The main character or characters find themselves in risky situations. There is an end goal or something they are trying to achieve, full of ups and downs. This genre is can be mixed with other genres.

Treasure Island, The Call of the Wild

CLASSICS

The classics have been around for ages and perhaps you've read them as assignments in English classes. They are generally great books with original ideas, which is why they stood the test of time. Many classics are well-known, so they have been used as references or inspiration for authors.

The Time Machine, Wizard of Oz

MYSTERY

The plot always revolves around a crime or issue. There is typically a main protagonist trying to solve the mystery and an antagonist who is eluding the protagonist. Most mysteries have some side stories that tie into the main plot, and twists are what draws readers in.

Nancy Drew, DaVinci Code

HISTORICAL FICTION

These books are based in a historical setting, but the stories are fiction. Historical fiction books are written as if they were real during certain historical events by conforming to cultural norms.

Gone with the Wind, Outlander

LITERARY FICTION

Like action and adventure, literary fiction is also a broad genre. Literary fiction is not just telling a story, but is the author stirring up emotions within the reader. The writer can do this by making the character or events relatable to the reader. This genre is very similar to drama.

Pride and Prejudice, To Kill a Mockingbird

Alerian Academy

Fantasy

Usually set in a fictional imagined world, many fantasy novels involve magic or the supernatural. Some fantasy could be based in the real world and involve fantasy elements. Many fantasy books provide details of the setting as readers must transport their imagination into a different world.

Lord of the Rings, Harry Potter

Horror

Horror is meant to cause fear for readers. Horror doesn't always have death or gore but it has been known to use the theme of something terrible or the unknown to cause fear. Horror stories can have supernatural elements. The most well-known horror authors include H.P. Lovecraft and Stephen King.

The Shining, Frankenstein

Graphic Novels

Also called comic books, graphic novels present a unique story through sequential artwork. They are presented in multiple panels per page and show strong emotions with interjections and speech bubbles. In many instances, graphic novels have a different writer and illustrator, making fans of comic books more dedicated to specific artists or writers within the same comic series. Although comic books have fewer words than a novel, they can tell a story of the same length because the pictures replace the visual details in a story.

Marvel, DC

Romance

Romance is self-explanatory. Although other genres may have romantic interests, the romance genre revolves around the romantic interest. Romance is the most widely sold genre and is the highest earning genre. Romance also has many different sub-genres, including contemporary, historical, paranormal, and erotica.

The Notebook, It Ends with Us

Science Fiction

Science fiction sets itself apart from other genres because they usually rely on technology and future science. This genre also includes topics like aliens and the apocalypse. Older sci-fi books such as dystopian novels are still labeled sci-fi even though the time period or technological advances have passed.

1984, Dune

SHORT STORIES

Short stories are generally just short novels. Many times, they can be combined in collections. In general, a short story should have less than 7,000 words. A novella should have less than 40,000 words.
Famous authors include the Grimm Brothers and Edgar Allen Poe

SUSPENSE OR THRILLERS

Suspense stories can resemble action, mystery, and even horror. This genre usually involves cliff angers and dangerous scenes. Typically, readers are left in the dark for many scenes and major reveals occur at random points within the story.
Girl with the Dragon Tattoo, Gone Girl

POETRY

Poetry is one of the genres where almost anything goes. Poetry in school is generally taught as rhyming words or lines with a certain rhythm or set of syllables, but poetry can evolve into all sorts of styles. Sometimes the message is straightforward, but other times, the poems speak in riddles or metaphors. The writer expects the reader to translate the meaning or feelings they are trying to convey.

A novel would be considered a fictional story. Sometimes the lines can get blurred in terms of fiction and non-fiction.

BIOGRAPHY

A biography is written as the chronological events of one's life. A biography is written by someone else. An autobiography is written by the person in the biography.

MEMOIR

Although similar to a biography, a memoir is usually a collection of short stories about the subject's life, such as significant accomplishments and hardships. They are generally meant to convey feelings or lessons to the reader.

TRUE CRIME

True crime books tell of actual crimes and events. Some readers may categorize true crime as novels. Even though based on real events, true crime does tell a story similar to that of a fiction novel.

Themes and Ideas

An author will choose a specific theme (or themes) along with the type of book to write. Multiple themes can be selected as sub-themes, but there should not be too many, otherwise, the book may veer off of the main plot and become confusing to the reader. More advanced authors may choose a theme later on in their writing process.

Love	Facing darkness	Man against nature
Hate	Family	Overcoming
Adventure	Fate and free will	Patriotism
Beauty	Self-preservation	Isolation
Change versus tradition	Technology	Power and corruption
Chaos and order	Good versus evil	Quest for discovery
Ambition	Heartbreak	Dreams
Discovery	Injustice	Displacement
Circle of life	Rebirth	Empowerment
Companionship	Heroism	Fear of failure
Convention and rebellion	Amusement	Fulfillment
Death	Superstition	Growing up
Quest for power	Individual versus society	Honor
Immortality	War	Vanity

Many themes go hand in hand. For example, *Island of the Blue Dolphins,* by Scott O'Dell, tells of a young girl who is left behind with her brother on an island. She is forced to grow up, survive, take care of her brother, and face the obstacles of the wildlife around her. This book obviously wouldn't have themes such as a quest for power or patriotism. Themes that would be included in this book would be self-preservation, man against nature, and companionship.

When themes are selected, characters, plots, and settings must match. The character cannot be a meek individual for a theme such as the quest for power. They would have to be strong, confident, and cunning. The setting of a theme involving chaos and order would probably include rebellion, a mismanaged society, and so on.

Audience

A theme and plot will go hand in hand with your audience. Your writing style, book cover, font size, adult topics, and much more go into finding a target audience. Marketing your novel will become much easier when understand who your readers will be.

Knowing your audience helps you know what to write. For example, books geared towards teens wouldn't include things like working to pay bills, adult content, and the struggle to maintain a household. On the other hand, a book written for adult audiences would have more significant words, advanced feelings, and maybe some adult content.

Who is going to read this book?

Think about what kind of audience your book is going to attract. Make the target audience specific according different factors such as age, gender, and lifestyle.

Who will be your secondary audience?

Although you will be writing for the enjoyment of your primary audience, it's always good to have secondary audiences in the back of your mind for marketing purposes.

Look at the competition.

Look for books that may be similar to yours. Look at your competing authors and their target audiences as well. This research can also give insight into font size, formatting, and book covers.

Connect.

Marketing your book to a certain audience in today's world is easily achieved through social media as well as personal connections. Certain websites are geared towards book reviews and recommendations. Social media helps attract your audiences with well-made shareable content. In a saturated book market, connecting to the audience is vital.

Children's books

Children's books are written specifically for children: fewer words, more pictures, and simple stories.

Young Adult (YA)

Young adult is a label for books read by pre-teen and teenage audiences. They are usually chapter books without adult themes, but still with intricate plots that are age appropriate.

Plot Outline

A plot will be your main story. Inspiration can hit anywhere and anytime. It could be from a dream, a conversation, or even a picture. Having a plot outline will help an author write their novel. You can make it as rough or as detailed as you want.

Status Quo

Rising Action

Climax

Falling action

Final Outcome

Status Quo: This is the start of the book. The story would start as a typical day before the incident.

The "Incident": The incident is what happens to disturb the status quo or the calm at the beginning of the book. It could be small or large, and the reader should feel that something exciting or an adventure is about to happen. Sometimes novels may start to when the day looks like after a certain event.

Developments: The developments, or rising action, make up the most significant part of the book. The main character will encounter obstacles. The development creeps up to the climax, and there can be some minor pitfalls during the rising action.

Climax: The climax is when the reader cannot put down the book. Something big is happening. It could be life or death or something not as intense, but this is a critical point in the book, and it doesn't last long.

Resolution: Your story needs to end in some way. It could be a number of things: sweet, sad, happy, or even leaving the reader with an open ending.

Subplots may also be added, but be careful, they should somehow fit into the main plot line. Having subplots that don't contribute to the main plot can be distracting.

Monomyth

A popular plot outline is the Hero's Journey. Joseph Campbell developed this plot line as a basic, but detailed version of the plot many books follow. The three main parts include **Separation**, **Initiation**, and the **Return**. Although many books may not follow the usual hero's journey, pieces can be taken to a novel for a loose interpretation.

Separation

THE DEPARTURE FROM THE KNOWN WORLD

The departure is something that disrupts the status quo. It can a be favorable or an unfavorable event The hero may choose to accept it willingly or choose to ignore it at first. Sometimes, the hero may not even know that the journey is starting.

THE CALL TO ADVENTURE

The Call to Adventure, or Call to Action, is when the protagonist has left and is starting his new journey after the disrupting event. The call can be signaled by a herald. For example a visit from Gandalf or a letter of invitation to Hogwarts after a certain age.

REFUSAL OF THE CALL

Sometimes, the hero refuses the call. Many times, they are uncomfortable or afraid. They may second-guess themselves or what is happening in the world around them. The refusal of the call can be temporary or permanent. When it is permanent, the hero eventually never goes on the journey. The refusal stage also may lay out the risks involved if the hero decided to go (or not go) on the journey.

MEETING WITH THE MENTOR

In almost every story, someone leads the way, maybe even multiple people. Think of Gandalf or Professor Dumbledore. They are usually old, wise, and willing to help the hero. The mentor can also be an inanimate object such as a map.

CROSSING THE FIRST THRESHOLD

The threshold is a new realm for the hero. They are unsure what will happen now that they are on the adventure. They have accepted what is to come.

Initiation

BELLY OF THE WHALE

The Belly of the Whale symbolizes the rebirth of the hero. The hero has to change themselves to face what is coming next. This is when he completely separates himself from what he knew before to completing the task at hand.

THE ROAD OF TRIALS

In the Trials, the hero is overcoming obstacles, tests, and challenges. Sometimes, they may be minuscule, but at other times, the trials may be so hard that the hero may think of giving up. The Road of Trials is very prevalent in the stories of Greek mythology. Aside from the main "quest", there may be mini quests or tests that the hero must go through.

MEETING WITH THE GODDESS

This is the point where the hero meets a "goddess". The word goddess may be in the image of a woman mentor, a lover, or a powerful being. Usually the goddess is the epitome of beauty and helps the hero along his way or is even a boon (gift) when the hero completes his journey. Sometimes this goddess can be an illusion, turning into the temptress in the next step of the hero's journey. The goddess can also represent the female side of the hero that will make him complete in the end.

Temptress

The temptress is not always a woman, but can be metaphorically something that is tempting the hero. The hero is tempted either by giving up his quest or sacrificing his morals. This is the part where the hero solidifies his will to finish his quest.

Atonement with the father

An analogy for when the hero finally understands that this current version of himself is what is needed to finish his adventure. The father may also be a symbol of the hero gaining approval of the father, he transforms from "childhood" and becomes a true adult.

Apotheosis

Right after the atonement, the hero realizes he is now divine. Apotheosis is the elevation of a person to the status of a god. The hero looks at the world from a different perspective because he now knows what kind of person to be to complete the journey. Gandalf the Grey transforming into Gandalf the White is an example of apotheosis.

The ultimate boon

The Boon is the gift that he receives from completing the quest. It can be anywhere from saving the world to finding a long-lost relative. The hero at this stage is also freed from whatever may have been holding him back such as fear, consequences, or desires.

Refusal of the return

The journey is over, but he may want to stay a hero instead of returning to his old life. The hero may want to stay in this new world that he has discovered or may have a fear of returning to the past world.

The magic flight

The hero usually will have to return home after his adventure is finished. He may have to leave something behind. The hero may receive something to help him return home. This would be something like *Wizard of Oz* where Dorothy is instructed to click her heels to return home.

Rescue from without

The characters who have helped him on his way have to help him back home. Sometimes the hero can be injured or need assistance either from those in his previous life or from those he had encountered on the journey.

Return

Crossing the return threshold

The hero returns home. This could be anywhere from being celebrated as a hero or not even wanting to be back.

Master of two worlds

The hero realizes that he is a better person by going on this adventure and that he had the ability to become a hero when he had doubted it in the beginning.

Freedom to live

The hero now lives a normal life but as a better person (or maybe worse).

Back to equilibrium

The story of the hero starts from the beginning as the status quo. The status quo may be externally the same as the beginning, but internally, the hero has changed.

The Hero's Journey

Character-Driven Journey

The following is a character-driven journey by Allen Palmer. Rather than focusing on events, this format focuses on the character and their own internal journey.

Incomplete	The protagonist is incomplete. This can be something they feel or something they are unaware of.
Unsettled	They are being called to action. They may accept or be reluctant; either way, they are unsettled because it's a significant change.
Resistant	The hero may feel reluctant to join this adventure. If the hero is not reluctant, people around him may be.
Encouraged	The protagonist is encouraged to go on the adventure. Although Campbell uses a mentor or supernatural power in this hero's journey, this encouragement can be anything.
Committed	They leave parts of themselves or turn away from the familiar to reach their quest.
Disoriented	The character faces challenges and people that can pull him in different directions.
Inauthentic	The hero has to go against his true behavior.
Confronted	The hero is confronted by his true flaws and he must change himself.
Reborn	The hero changes himself to continue the quest.
Desperate	There are complications during the adventure or maybe even self-sabotage.
Decisive	The climax of the story when the hero finally wins.
Complete	The hero feels complete by navigating whatever had made them feel incomplete in the beginning.

Character Driven

Because Allen Palmer's Hero's Journey is character-driven, it can be applied without involving fantasy or outside elements into the story.

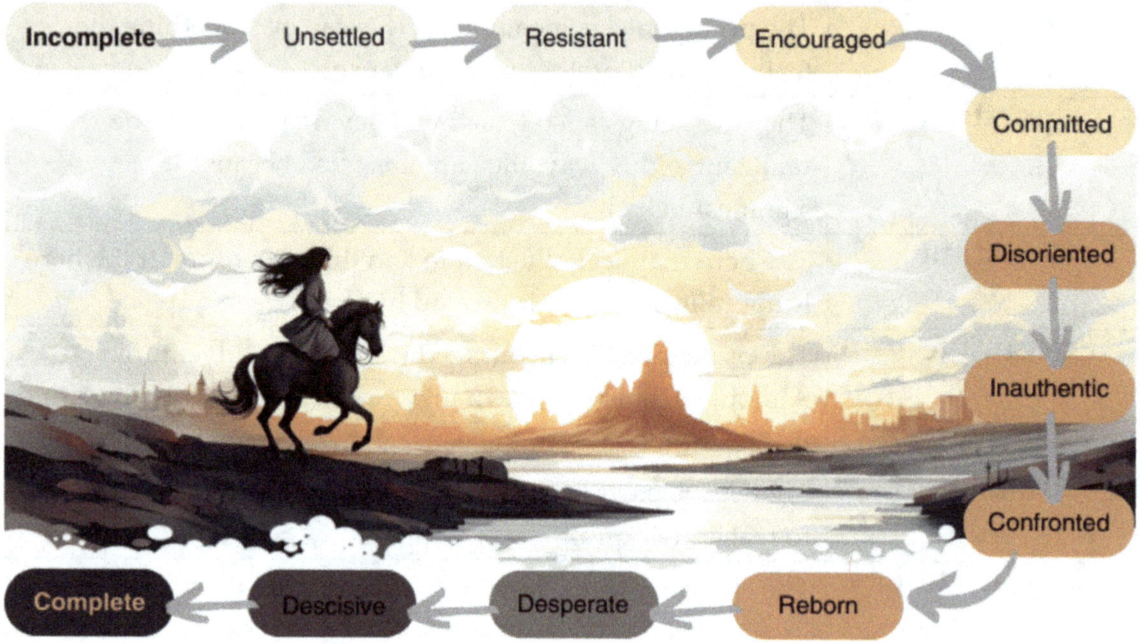

Although the character journey can skip a few steps or have some parts out of order, the messages usually includes:

- An incomplete person
- Being called to a higher purpose
- Obstacles
- Hard decisions
- Completion

Characters

Character development is the art of being a writer but also a psychologist and sociologist. A novel should be made up of entirely believable people.

Characters are based on reality. Honest reactions and real-life problems in a novel are realistic and must be believable to the reader. Remember, people can't relate to very unrealistic characters.

A hero is presented in many novels, especially fantasy novels, and so are sidekicks, mentors, and villains, most of them follow similar paths. Characters are usually predefined as the protagonist, the antagonist, the mentor, the ally, and the love interest.

Can there be more than one person in every character-type category? Yes, but remember that having several antagonists and protagonists may make your book too hard to understand. You'll also have random characters in your book, but having random characters that don't tie into the book makes little sense and clogs up the reader's memory of who is who.

Think of characters in novel writing as a movie. Opening credits have only a few names written as prominent characters in a movie. Other than the extras walking in the streets or shopping at the store, you only see a handful of people in films with a significant amount of speaking lines.

Creating a baseline character is easy. Look at those around you, the person at the bank, or even at yourself. **Everyone is as unique as a book character; your job is to help a reader visualize and understand them.**

Antagonist and Protagonist

Usually branded "the good guy" and "the bad guy", or "the hero" and "the villain", but that's not always the case when it comes to creating an antagonist and a protagonist.

The protagonist is the main character in a story. The plot is developed around the protagonist, while the **antagonist is the character that generally works against the main character**. The antagonist can come in many different forms other than a typical villain. There may be several antagonists, all with varying degrees of importance.

Some antagonists are not necessarily the bad guys. They are called **conflict creators**. They may even be relatable, but their goals are opposite and work against the protagonist. Some examples of antagonists who aren't necessarily bad guys are Willy Wonka and the government in *E.T.*

Sometimes, the antagonist in a story isn't even a person.
In *The Perfect Storm*, the storm and the ocean are natural antagonists.
In *The Island of the Blue Dolphins*, the wild dogs are antagonists.
Even the supernatural, such as the shine in *The Shining*, would be considered an antagonist.
The protagonist can also be their own antagonist.

- Don't make your characters too weak or too strong. If readers know the outcome of the conflict because one is obviously stronger than the other, readers may get bored.
- Create and write both the antagonist and protagonist in a relatable way.
"I kind of get where the bad guy is coming from."
- Just because they are the antagonists doesn't mean they are entirely unrelatable. Remember, bad guys can have goals, aspirations, and positive traits too.
- Novels can have more than one protagonist and antagonist, but writing in more than one may cause chaos for the reader and for the storyline..

The Anti-Hero

An antihero is generally an antagonist or a main character who, unlike heroes, may have deep flaws or are similar to villains.

Usually, the anti-hero is a deep and well-thought-out character that the readers may relate to. Unlike the traditional hero, they can be social outcasts, have a shady past, are morally compromised, or reject authority. Still, an anti-hero has a goal in common with the hero. How they achieve this goal or view it can be completely different.

Anti-heroes are complex, have internal conflict, a consistent moral compass (lines they do not cross), but most of all, they are NOT the villain.

Things that can be included with anti-hero character creation
- thorough backstory on why they behave the way they do
- sense of justice for vigilantes
- self-preservation
- moral issues and hard decisions
- relatable flaws
- self-serving nature
- living in a gray area/lines they don't cross
- cultural impacts/how society has affected them
- questionable methods
- motives and end goals
- some good characteristics that shine through
- sidekicks
- temptations
- their own logic

Think of characters in Greek mythology, the original anti-heroes.

Zeus - Wisdom and abilities, bad at marriage and having friends.
Aphrodite - Loving and romantic, jealous and conceited
Athena - Strong and helpful, lack of compassion and lust for vengeance

Greek gods being anti-heroes are what made them so appealing in stories because of the relatable human connection.

Anti-Hero Types

Classic Anti-Hero

A classic anti-hero is someone who is reaching an end goal of heroism but is morally compromised. They have deep character flaws, but the reader still cheers them on.

Unwilling Anti-Hero

Some anti-heroes are thrust into a story similar to that of a hero, but unlike the hero, the anti-hero tries to back out whenever possible. They complain loudly and often.

The Pragmatic

The rebellious anti-hero still follows the hero's journey, but they are realistic about it. Not everything will be sunshine and rainbows, and some villains may need to be physically persuaded for the anti-hero to get the point across.

Unscrupulous Anti-Hero

One type of anti-hero may include one whose self-interests drive them. They are flawed humans but can show good intentions, just not by following the rules.

Vigilantes

Vigilantes may do all that is possible to become the hero. They see their actions as no choice other than to do bad things for the greater good or for justice. The police and authorities are limited by red tape, therefore vigilantes must take matters into their own hands.

Severus Snape, James Bond, Geralt of Rivia, Han Solo, Wolverine, Robin Hood, and Catwoman are all anti-heroes with different motivations, morals, and flaws.

Common Character Types

Type		Example 1	Example 2
The Hero	The hero is the main protagonist. They are taking the journey.	Harry Potter	Frodo
The Villain	The antagonist is working against the protagonist. Villains, like heroes, can also be more than one.	Voldemort	Sauron
The Sidekicks	Sidekicks generally make up more than one person.	Ron Hermoine	Sam, Aragorn Legolas, Gimli
Villain Sidekicks	Villains need henchmen that create more conflict.	Wormtail Bellatrix	Saruman Nazgul
The Love Interest	Doesn't always have to be the love interest of the hero.	Ginny	Arwen
The Mentor	Usually in the form of an old man and carries wisdom from age and experience.	Dumbledore	Gandalf
The Nurturer	Usually a mother figure. Typically is wise and has life experience with good advice..	McGonagall Molly Weasley	Galadriel
The Jester	Usually, characters that are likable but mess things up in the story.	Hagrid	Merry Pippin
The Shapeshifter	Someone who's identity and true intentions are not completely known.	Snape	Gollum

Jungian Archetypes

Carl Jung created the 12 archetypes of people. These archetypes are basic patterns that are part of the collective unconscious. They also incorporate social and personal behavior.

Type	Goal	Fear	Flaw
Hero	Change World	Weakness	Tunnel vision
Creator	Realize Vision	Mediocrity	Unfinished projects
Lover	Connection	Isolation	Objectification
Rebel	Revolution	No Power	Habitual destruction
Caregiver	Help Others	Selfishness	Rescue the wrong people
Explorer	Freedom	Entrapment	Wanderlust
Jester	Fun	Boredom	No responsibility
Sage	Knowledge	Deception	Unempathetic
Orphan	Belonging	Exclusion	Taken advantage of easily
Magician	Alter Reality	Unintended Results	Manipulation
Ruler	Prosperity	Overthrown	Controlling
Innocent	Happiness	Punishment	Naive

Alerian Academy

Character Layout Questions

The following are base questions for characters that are pretty important to a story. Even though you may not end up using all the information, it is useful to know the character as well as you do your best friend.

By knowing what kind of people they are, a writer should be able to answer these questions with clues within the story.

What do they look like?
How do they act?
What are their ambitions?
What is their occupation?
How do they act in society?
What kind of past do they have?
What are their likes and dislikes?
How do they react?
Are they an introvert or extrovert?
Do they have any triggers?
Who are their friends?
Where do their loyalties lie?
What worries do they have?
Do they have any weird quirks?
How intelligent are they?
Do they have physical abnormalities?
What kind of family life do they have?
Are they a leader or follower?

After some basic character creation, you can go into smaller details that make them unique.

Coffee or tea?
T-shirt or polo?
What kind of car do they drive?
Are they able to touch their toes?
What is their favorite school subject?
What is their pain tolerance?
Early riser or night owl?

Think of how to keep track of your characters so your novel is consistent.

Setting

The setting is when and where the story takes place.

There are three main aspects to the setting of a novel: **Place**, **time**, and **environment**.

The place is vital and there are many degrees of "places". A conversation taking place in a living room is a place, and so is the house that the living room is in. That house will be located in a neighborhood in a particular city or district. This city may be in a state, in a country on a continent, and finally, on a planet nobody has heard of because your novel isn't set on Earth.

Time can include a historical point in time or even just the time of day. Seasons, a certain month, or holiday can even play a significant role in the novel.

Although we may think that the place would be directly linked to the environment, there are many factors that make up an environment.

usual or unusual jobs	physical location	public sentiments
neighborhoods	politics	beliefs
family values	climate	crises
social groups	weather	cultural surroundings
community	social norms	historical context

There are different levels of importance in a setting. Stories can give a general location such as a neighborhood or school, even without mentioning a particular city. This method focuses on a story rather than the setting. Other stories may use the setting around them to tell the story.

BACKDROP SETTING

Sometimes, the setting is barely mentioned. This would be considered a backdrop setting. The story can happen anytime or anywhere. The story itself is generally more important than where or how. Readers can usually relate to a story with a backdrop setting, however, novels rarely have a complete backdrop setting as opposed to short stories.

INTEGRAL SETTING

An integral setting is used when the time and place are essential to the story. Integral settings are crucial for some types of stories. For example, a historical setting or a futuristic sci-fi setting will have a direct impact to the story. In a historical setting, characters will have to ride on horses, write letters, and maybe use a gas lamp. In a futuristic setting, characters may have hoverboards, telepathic communication, and retinal security systems to enter their homes. Another important part of the integral setting is the culture and traditions held in different regions of the world. A story of a girl from the Midwest will lead a completely different life than a girl in Hong Kong.

In the novel, *My Side of Mountain*, Sam learns how to survive in the Catskill Mountains in upstate New York. Leaving his family home in the cities, he sets off to find his old family farm. Sam spends months in the wilderness learning to survive in his surroundings. This book places significant importance on the setting as he is required to interact with the wilderness. In this book, the changing of the seasons is essential to how Sam survives. Another influential part of the story setting is the expansion of New York into the mountains.

"Imagination is like a muscle. I found out that the more I wrote, the bigger it got."

Philip José Farmer

Expansion

Action and Adventure

Action and adventure stories have been around for centuries. The most famous ancient stories come from those based on mythology, Homer being the most well-known ancient storyteller.

An action and adventure story can have elements of a mystery or thriller. Action and adventure, while not exactly the same, will have a similar outline that generally follows the hero's journey.

An adventure is not point A to point B, but the journey to all the places in between.

Essential things you need for an action or adventure story:

A Hero

The main character of an action-adventure story will most often start as an ordinary person before they embark on their adventure. Don't be afraid to create an anti-hero.

A Villain

One or more "bad guys" increases the stakes. Depending on the story, the protagonists are one step ahead or one step behind the antagonist.

A Vital Ignition

Make an event or catalyst that dramatically changes the hero's life. This ignition starts the plot and gets the ball rolling on the adventure.

A Quest

The protagonist will be presented with a problem they must solve.

An Environment

The environment will change; this can be a situation or a place. It is typically something unfamiliar to the hero.

Stakes and Risk

In an adventure story, the character who opposes the antagonist usually encounters danger and difficulties. The adventure may put lives at risk. More risks should be placed intentionally throughout the novel. Place a countdown of when the hero will "lose". Create some setbacks and elevate the risks.

A Transformation

Throughout their journey, the main character goes through trials that change the hero for the better (maybe even worse).

Supporting Characters

Use supporting characters as sidekicks or mentors. It's challenging to write action if there is only a protagonist involved in the action. Think of spy movies, where some geeky scientists in the background help the antagonist achieve their goal.

Pace

Readers don't like feeling bogged down with slow parts in an action novel. Outline plot points and vital events. Keep the story moving without slowing down, but don't rush the reader either.

Mystery

Mysteries are widely one of the most popular genres of books for all ages, whether it's a novel about a triple homicide or about who ate Sally's cookies. They are written in a way where **the reader feels like they are working with the protagonist to solve the mystery**.

The earliest detective story is *"The Murders of Rue Morgue"* by Edgar Allen Poe, published in a magazine in 1841. The first mystery novel was *"The Woman in White"* by Wilkie Collins, published in 1859. In 1868, *"The Moonstone"* was considered the first detective novel.

The most popular series of detective books is *Sherlock Holmes* by Sir Arthur Conan Doyle, enough to be a household name and the protagonist of several movies and TV shows.

Mysteries are based on a crime or a puzzle, sometimes a series of them. The stakes are high, and the mystery is generally time-based, elevating the risk. The protagonists aren't always detective and law enforcement, as seen in *Nancy Drew* and *The Hardy Boys*.

The setting and the style of the mystery can vary greatly. While some mysteries may feature a busy city, some may be based on the quiet countryside. Some mystery novels may be dark and serious, others may take comedic approaches. They can be written in both the first and third person, but **keep in mind what information should be revealed to the reader to keep the story exciting and mysterious.**

- Use logic and intuition throughout the novel.

- Use human psychology and sociology.

- Have a great first chapter that draws the reader in.

- Give clues in a timely manner.

- Focus on the details of the plotline and subplots so there are no plot holes.

- Don't make solving the crime too obvious.

- Drop slight hints that might be missed.

- Think of any plot twist or misleading information.

- Add in conflict.

- Create characters that would be believable in their abilities to be able to solve the mystery.

- Do research on how crimes can be committed so they are believable.

Graphic Novels

Although similar in style, graphic novels and comics are not quite the same.

Think of **graphic novels as movies; comics are more like TV shows.**

Comics are generally "by chapter" and usually printed in thin volumes on paper, similar to newspaper material. Comics are not just superheroes in booklets, but are also in newspapers featuring Garfield and Marmaduke.

Graphic novels generally have a start and end to a story and are usually printed on high-quality paper, similar to high-end magazines. Some graphic novels can even be a series of comics rolled into one.

Manga is another type of graphic novel created in Japan. Most well-known comics in America cycle through different artists and writers with intellectual property belonging to companies like DC and Marvel. Manga usually belongs to a creator and employs a group of assistants, which is why manga stays consistent with style and storytelling, as comics generally have variables in art and storytelling.

Before writing a graphic novel or comic, **knowing your audience is essential**, as they can vary widely in content and artwork. While comics and graphic novels can have intense or gruesome art, comics such as Garfield and Peanuts appeal to all audiences. It is also important to know if you will create a graphic novel (stand-alone story) or a comic with a series.

The artwork is one of the most important aspects of graphic novels and comics. In addition to having a good story, the artwork must be visually appealing for readers. A great story might be ruined by less-than-appealing art. While there technically isn't a wrong or right to artwork, it may be good to study styles with critiques to best match the audience's expectations. Readers will read not only the text but the art as well.

Make sure your panels flow in an easy-to-read format. Although panels tend to read left to right, up to down, there are many variations of how to read a comic book, as most pages won't adhere to a single specific layout. The more variations of panels and alignments may look attractive but also can cause confusion.

Graphic novels are edgy and intense, filled with suspense and action. Usually, they involve impossible and unusual situations. Keep to a storyline to help balance out the timing of the story and to know what artwork should accompany the story. Stick to only the important parts of the story, and don't add unnecessary parts.

Literary Fiction

Literary fiction is often a style very closely related to what one would consider "literature". The books assigned in high school and college that students must write summaries and philosophical entries within their own translations of books are often those found in the literary fiction category.

Literary fiction is usually thematic along the lines of being almost entirely character-driven. In literary fiction, there could not be any real hero, climax, or actual plot in place, as it is mainly driven by physiological and sociological plotlines. The story has no formula, so happy endings and resolutions may not even be present.

Literary fiction places greater emphasis on the characters themselves rather than following a regular story structure. This creates a more serious undertone of character valuation.

The genre also is set apart by the style of writing. Metaphors, similes, and symbolism play an important role in literary fiction more than other genres to tell a story. Creative ways to explain details and the use of big uncommon words have been labeled by many critics as being "snobbish".

One way to look at literary fiction is to compare it to other genres in terms of movies. Many films that receive Oscars are generally slow dramas only released in certain theaters and have a specific artistic touch. On the other hand, box-office hits that make millions in profits and have action-figure contracts are generally films that won't receive film awards. Literary fiction generally isn't extremely popular or high-earning, but it fits within a category of high literature.

Literary fiction has had many critiques, such as *"Literary fiction is an artificial luxury brand, but it doesn't sell."*-Damien Walter and popular writers calling the genre dull and stagnant. Fans of literary fiction give praise to style and tone.

On the other hand, it's known that books that may not fit into a particular genre are set into the category of literary fiction, making the genre essentially fluid.

Romance

Romance is statistically the most popular and highest-earning genre in America, even though more than 80% of the readers are women.

Two main ideas are needed for a romance novel: a **central love story and a satisfying ending,**

In general, romance novels will have the love story in common, but beyond that, any plot and style is acceptable, making this genre adaptable to many audiences and can have many subgenres. More than a quarter of novels are romance, and with the number of romance novels being published yearly, creative plotlines have entered the sales stream. Anywhere from mafia romance to arranged marriages, have had its own cult following through social media.

Contemporary Romance: Romance novels that are set in the present day. The time period would typically be from the end of World War II to the present day. Modern romance books could include things like dating apps and technology.

Historical Romance: Romance novels set during or before World War II. Conducting research is vital for this subgenre to be culturally accurate because romance and courtship were vastly different than what it is now.

Erotic Romance: Erotic romances, known as smut, are explicit in nature, containing erotic and sexual scenes. One has to care for the audience and their preferred balance between sexual scenes and plot. Within this genre, many subgenres may wander into regions of kink or danger.

Young Adult Romance: Romance novels geared towards younger readers. These books don't feature erotic scenes and are typically written in a coming-of-age viewpoint.

Other romance genres can include Amish Romance, Dark Romance, Paranormal Romance.

Horror

The genre of horror is to illicit some sort of fear or dread in a reader. This could be from imagery, gore, and even psychological effects.

The atmosphere is vital to a good horror story, whether dark and unknown territories or a happy suburban neighborhood with something seriously wrong in the background.

Horror has some subgenres, but the uniqueness of horror is finding something that an audience can be scared of. Monsters and the supernatural can be scary, but even more streamlined things, such as killer clowns and toys that come to life, can also be used.

Historically, horror stemmed from ancient times with writings about the devil, evil spirits, and demons. Horror also was prevalent in Greek mythology.

Many horror stories stem from adaptations of classic books.

Frankenstein by Mary Shelley

Strange Case of Dr. Jekyll and Mr. Hyde by Robert Louis Stevenson

Dracula by Bram Stoker

H.P. Lovecraft, an undeniable influence in horror, said *"The oldest and strongest emotion of mankind is fear, and the oldest and strongest kind of fear is fear of the unknown."*

Stephen King, one of the most well-known horror novelists, has had many of his books turned into movies, and they have have been prominent due to their spooky nature, mostly of the unknown.

RL Stine, the creator of *Goosebumps,* found his niche in children's horror.

In horror, it's essential to understand psychology and sociology. Novels differ vastly from film because books cannot introduce jump scares or certain visuals. On the other hand, novels can describe thoughts and feelings that aren't easily displayed in film.

Alerian Academy

Suspense and Thriller

Suspense and thrillers may be great to watch in the movies, but writing a thriller may be challenging for some. Like action and adventure, pacing is essential in a thriller. Even though a mystery, action, and thriller may seem the same, there are some notable differences.

Mystery: The story progresses because of the protagonist rather than the situation or environment. Clues are generally uncovered steadily as thrillers tend to ebb and flow for dramatic effect. Usually, the person who committed the crime is uncovered at the end. Thrillers can take the opposite role, with the reader knowing who the antagonist is from the beginning, reading the protagonist who is trying to stop the antagonist from completing their end goal.

Action: In an action novel, the story isn't always filled with emotions and unlike thrillers or suspense, can elicit happy feelings. A thriller is suspenseful, and readers don't know what's coming next from the authors creative use of unexpected twists and turns.

Horror: Thrillers elicit suspense and thrill, while horror is meant to scare. Instead of using tension, horror will use the psychological effects of fear. Horror generally doesn't have the same amount of action scenes of that a thriller.

When writing thrillers, the author must know when to excite the pace and when to drag things out. Emotions are brought up by not knowing whether something big will happen soon.

Characters will always matter in novels, but in a thriller, it is usually the situation and environment that must be thought out.

Like an action, thrillers must use high stakes, but the stakes can change, by the situation constantly changing because of external factors in the formation of plot twists and obstacles.

Tension is key. Instead of violence that may be never-ending, thrillers focus on the impending violence.

Biography and Memoir

Biographies, autobiographies, and memoirs are about a specific person's life, but there are key differences to each style.

A **biography** is a story about someone's life, whether from childhood to adulthood or specific events throughout their lives. The book isn't written by the subject, making the biography a third-person point of view. Biographies are a little more formal than a memoir or an autobiography and are written as non-fiction surrounded by facts rather than emotions. In many cases, the biography is written without the subject's consent. This can create legal problems for those subjects who are still alive.

In an **autobiography**, the author is the subject of the story, so the book is told from the first-person point of view. Autobiographies are classified as creative nonfiction, although some autobiographies come under fire for not being entirely truthful about events. Also, unlike biographies, autobiographies include emotions and not just facts. Since the author is generally not a writer, they often employ someone to work with for the book to be written seamlessly. Autobiographies will also include details that won't be found in research and will often present new information or points of view to the reader.

Memoirs are similar to autobiographies but much more relatable to collections of stories. The memoirs are not based on important events but on events that are important to the author. This could be a story about a specific summer where nothing noteworthy may have happened, but it may have been a time of great revelation for the author.

For a biography, one must conduct research. Public or individual sources can provide different information. However, one must be very careful because a biography should be the same as non-fiction, where the facts should always be truthful. The author may also seek out permission from the subject. This creates a relationship where the subject may reveal events that are not public information and also create a safety net for the author.

As for writing an autobiography, the author should have a great memory of what they were feeling during specific events. Sometimes, an autobiography will include childhood stories that shape how the author behaves and reacts.

Writing memoirs is all about feelings; therefore, it could be easier to write as things that happened in the past that affected the author will most likely be the easiest to write. Psychologically, this may be the easiest to write and remember, but the author must make sure that the content is relevant and relatable. There must be dramatic moments as well as light-hearted moments to draw empathy from the audience. Even though the memoir is not fiction, it should read similarly to fiction.

Poetry

Poetry can come in many different shapes and sizes. Rhyming, syllables, and lines are rules for certain poems, while some poems may seem sporadic without any form or structure. While poetry itself will not be a novel, there are entire books made up of collections of poems.

SONNET

This type of poetry was developed in Italy and was famously used by William Shakespeare. Sonnets are 14 lines and typically English sonnets are ABAB CDCD EFEF GG.

ODE

Odes are an ancient form of poetry used to praise a person, thing, or event.

ELEGY

Elegies are all about death.

BALLAD

In a poetic sense, ballads usually tell a dramatic story in four-line stanzas. Ballads are also considered to be the groundwork for modern music.

ACROSTIC

Acrostics are a play on words with letters. A word is word spelled vertically, and a specific word is written horizontally for every letter. In general, the words correspond to a certain message or theme.

VILLANELLE

Originating in France, this type of poetry has 19 lines, five parts with three lines, and the last with four. The rhyme is ABA ABA ABA ABA ABA ABAA.

HAIKU

Haikus consist of just three lines. The first and third lines have five syllables, while the second has seven. Haikus are usually written about nature.

Free VERSE

Free verse is a free-for-all, anything-goes style.

LIMERCK

Limericks are generally vulgar. The rhymes are AABBA. The A rhyme lines are typically longer than the B lines.

Other poetry styles include Ekphrastic, Sestina, Lyric, Ghazal, Erasure/Blackout, Epics, Narrative, Pantoum, Prose, Epitaph, Palindrome, List, Echo Verse.

Short Stories

Short stories are precisely what the title implies. The main difference between short stories and novels is the word count.

Short story elements contain the same formulas as a novel.

Short stories may be popular for those who know they don't have much time to devote to books or for those aware that their attention span may not be great for long novels. For authors and publishers, a short story is usually cheaper to print, providing a cost benefit.

Short stories, however, can lack certain elements that make the story enjoyable for some readers. Subplots are taken out, and there may be a lack of character development. Some descriptive details will have to be left out, and the reader may think the story is flat.

Sir Arthur Conan Doyle created *Sherlock Holmes* that are comprised of 56 short stories.

There are generally four categories of books that are categorized by word counts.

Short story - under 10,000

Novelette - 7,500-17,000

Novella - 10,000 - 40,000

Novel - More than 40,000 (but the average is 70,000 - 120,000)

Factors also include if the book is geared toward YA. Even *Harry Potter* has dramatic variances in word count.

Sorcerer's Stone - 76,944

Chamber of Secrets - 85,141

Prisoner of Azkaban - 107,253

Goblet of Fire - 190,637

Order of the Phoenix - 257,045

Half-Blood Prince - 168,923

Deathly Hallows - 198,227

Alerian Academy

True Crime

True crime is essentially a non-fiction story read like a fiction book. Although things may be embellished, the story and events leading up to the ending must be true.

Most true crime authors are ex-law enforcement (or even current officials) who turned to writing because of the size or relevance of the case. Some may also be writers who chronicled a particular case that had been substantially covered by the news and had taken up the role of an investigative journalist.

In a true crime novel, the plot may have strange or even nonsensical turn of events but the story is based on actual events. Some parts may have to be assumed because pieces do not always fit together in real-life scenarios.

Research is critical in true crime. People who followed the case may discredit the book if they feel as if they have been lied to about the events. Authors have advised that researching any actual crime or mystery involves attending court hearings, visiting institutions, or even taking a peek at crime scenes.

If the author was part of the investigation, they will need to decide how to present themselves (first or third person), and how much of themselves and their role or personal life to put into the book.

Science Fiction

Science fiction is dependent on technology or the future. Technology is an ever-changing and progressing part of our lives, so it would make sense that it would be a genre.

There are two categories of science fiction. **Hard science fiction** and **soft science fiction**.

Hard science fiction is comparable to an integral setting where the story depends on the technology around them. Soft science fiction is more like a backdrop setting of technology, where they may live in a world of technological advances, but it's not as important as the story itself. While many science fiction categories lie somewhere in between, most will lean one way or another.

Some dystopian books are heavily reliant on a science fiction backdrop. Almost all books that deal with space exploration would be science fiction. All books involving robots that take over the world would be considered science fiction.

There are many varying opinions on the degrees of science fiction and what it all entails.

When writing science fiction, the setting revolves around a time, place, and social structure where technology has developed enough to be relevant in the book. It is imperative to take a thoughtful approach to what has changed technologically. For example, would you have flying cars at a time when people would still be using flip phones? This is up to the author's creativity, but it still has to make sense to the audience.

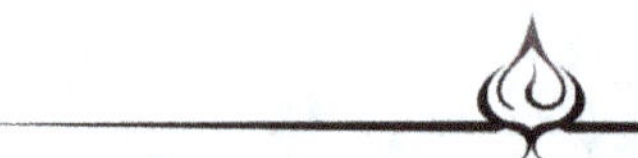

Historical Setting

A historical setting can be used in your novel, but unlike a more present environment, you may need to do significant amount of research for the time period to use in your story to feel authentic.

Landscape: Make sure your landscape and civic development fit historically. For example, *Little House on the Prairie* was written when people were still settling across the plains. There were seldom any bustling cities, just a lot of rolling hills and grass.

Social Constructs: Mannerisms historically change over time. Things widely accepted now may not have been before, and vice-versa. This includes clothing and things that have since gone out of style. Mannerisms and attitudes towards specific ideas such as marriage and occupations all have to be considered and reflected within the novel.

Technology: Technology is an integral part of history and must be researched as well. Ford's Model T was not mass-produced until 1913, the first lighter was made in 1823, and Google was founded in 1998. Looking up when glass windows were in production may help you with an early English historical setting.

Political climate: Politics, laws and government used to be wildly different back then. Think back to the days when you could be thrown in jail and executed in a matter of days or when "the crown" would raise taxes for a war. Although government systems have always been in place, the systems back then were completely different. Think of the Wild West where lawlessness may have been rampant in an area that only had a couple of law enforcement officials.

Setting Location List

Think of where your characters are. Details and specific locations are vital to the reader's imagination.

expanse	butte	swamp	river	pit
landscape	canyon	wetland	runoff	quarry
outback	cliff		sea	rift
seascape	highland	cove	shore	shaft
wilderness	hills	backwater	spring	sinkhole
brush	ledge	bank	strait	trench
bush	mesa	bay	stream	void
forest	mountain	beach	waterfall	earthworks
jungle	pass	brackish	watering-hole	mound
rainforest	peak	brook	waterway	remains
woods	plateau	channel	well	ruins
clearing	ridge	cistern	archipelago	country
farmland	ridgeline	coast	atoll	county
field	summit	creek	island	domain
grassland	lava fields	delta	isle	dominion
grove	volcano	falls	isthmus	duchy
meadow	crater	Fjord	peninsula	earldom
pasture	glen	fountain	reef	empire
plains	gorge	geyser	sandbar	kingdom
prairie	gully	gulf		land
savannah	hollow	inlet	abyss	nation
desert	ravine	lagoon	cave	principality
dunes	vale	lake	cavern	province
sands	valley	oasis	chasm	realm
wasteland	bayou	ocean	crack	shire
glacier	bog	pond	darkness	state
iceberg	flood plain	pool	depths	
tundra	marsh	rapids	hole	
bluff	moor	reservoir	mine	

abbey	citadel	hamlet	metropolis	shrine
academy	city	harbor	mill	slum
alley	cloister	hermitage	monastery	square
amphitheater	college	hideaway	mosque	stable
apothecary	colosseum	hideout	museum	stadium
aquarium	commune	highway	nest	street
arena	conservatory	hold	nunnery	stronghold
armory	convent	homestead	observatory	synagogue
asylum	coop	hospital	orchard	tabernacle
avenue	cottage	house	outbuilding	tavern
bakery	court	hovel	outpost	temple
bar	courthouse	hut	palace	tenement
barn	courtyard	inn	parish	tent
barracks	crossroad	intersection	park	tepee
baths	crypt	jail	path	terrace
battlefield	dam	junction	pen	tomb
bazaar	den	keep	plaza	town
beacon	dike	kennel	port	track
boulevard	ditch	laboratory	prison	trail
brewery	dock	labyrinth	pub	treasury
brothel	dump	lair	ranch	trenches
burrow	dungeon	landmark	repository	university
cabin	encampment	lean-to	retreat	vault
camp	estate	library	road	villa
campsite	fairground	lighthouse	roost	village
campus	farm	lodge	route	vineyard
canal	forge	longhouse	safehouse	warehouse
castle	fort	lumber yard	sanctuary	way
catacombs	fortress	madhouse	sanctum	wharf
cathedral	foundry	manor	sawmill	wigwam
cellar	garden	manse	settlement	windmill
cemetery	ghetto	mansion	sewer	workshop
chapel	grave	marina	shack	yurt
chateau	graveyard	marketplace	shelter	zoo
church	greenhouse	mausoleum	shipwreck	
circus	gutter	maze	shipyard	

Fantasy

Fantasy is one of the most creative ways to make a setting because almost anything goes. Rules of the regular world can be changed and manipulated without consequence. Whether a part of the story or not, the reader must understand the rules of this fantasy world with thoughtful writing.

Fantasy does not always mean dragons and fairies. **Fantasy is manipulating the world around us**, but a writer must carefully explain to the reader the new rules of the universe.

There can be many levels to a fantasy-based novel. A novel based on pirates may have the riches and the thrill of treasure and the open seas. Pirates are not made up, as we still have them in the present day in some capacity. The pirates in stories are dressed in stripes, have a hat, a peg-leg perhaps, an eye patch, and a macaw on a shoulder.   Although based on some real-life events and people, pirates would be considered fantasy to an extent.

Primary Worlds - Low Fantasy

A primary world is set in our world but with some different rules. Usually, the immediate world has hidden elements like magic or fantasy creatures. The fantasy elements are usually secret from the rest of the muggles.

Secondary Worlds - High Fantasy

A secondary world is an entirely new fantasy realm. Extensive details must be presented to the reader as countries, people, politics, language, time, and any rules of the universe can be changed or manipulated.

Fantasy Sub-Genres

PORTAL FANTASY

Portal fantasy is when the book starts off in the primary world and stumbles upon the secondary world. Usually, these books have a villain that the main character must beat to get back to the immediate world.

ANTHROPOMORPHIC FANTASY

The anthropomorphic fantasy involves talking animals. Although most talking animals are generally short stories for children, there are novels with animals that are used to convey a message.

PARANORMAL FANTASY

Paranormal fantasy, usually set in a primary world that includes creatures and people such as vampires, witches, and werewolves.

HISTORICAL FANTASY

Historical fantasy is set within a historical time period. Although some events may be real, elements such as magic can be added.

MYTHOLOGICAL FANTASY

Mythological fantasy draw their worlds and characters from mythology, most commonly Greek mythology. Since mythological stories has already established characters and their personalities, it is the job of the writer to create stories along the lines of what the actual mythological characters would do.

SCIENCE FANTASY

A science fantasy, different than science fiction will usually present itself as technological and magical.

MAGICAL REALISM

Magical realism is similar to a primary world fantasy, except the fantasy elements are not hidden. Magic is fully acknowledged and accepted by the people of the primary world. This can also include superhero fantasy.

Although this many seem like a comprehensive list of fantasy sub-genres, there are many more sub-genres that give more detail such as cyberpunk, paranormal romance, and contemporary fantasy.

Primary World
Low Fantasy

Also called low fantasy, primary worlds are built around our regular world with magical elements that are hidden to society.

The Green Mile by Stephen King, turned movie starring Tom Hanks, is about an inmate locked up for the murders of two young girls. The story is the retelling of the inmate through the guard's memories. The accused is a man who later shows that he has healing and empath abilities.

Although it could be likened to a portal fantasy, the plot of *Harry Potter* revolves around a primary fantasy world built into modern England and Scotland. The platform 9 3/4 is a portal itself, but it is neither something you stumble into nor something that just appeared. The magical element of going into the realm of magic is made to conceal the wizarding world. If this were portal fiction, the magic would stay in the magical realm and not appear in the ordinary world. Instead of another world or parallel universe, Harry Potter deals in an embedded world where magic and charms hide the wizarding world away from the "muggles".

Things in Harry Potter that give hints to the magic being concealed in the real world as opposed to a portal fantasy:

The snake at the zoo talks to Harry in Parceltongue.

Hermoine's parents are muggles, yet she is a witch.

The Prime Minister in the real world is in touch and aware of the Ministry of Magic.

Other magic schools are located in real-world countries.

There are protocols in place (Statute of Secrecy) to help conceal the existence of witchcraft.

In *Mary Poppins*, a seemingly ordinary family is in the presence of a nanny who can use magic. Famous for her floating umbrella and animated manipulations, Mary Poppins has several abilities that she denies she has.

Secondary World
High Fantasy

High fantasy involves works where the whole world in the novel is fabricated. The rules of the world can be changed; however, this comes at a price. Loopholes are often found in many high fantasy novels, so it's recommended to get all the stories straight while writing a high fantasy.

The most famous high fantasy novel series was written by J.R.R. Tolkien from 1937 to 1949. Like most epic novels, it became a series of several books. While many books simply make a fantasy world, Tolkien developed an entire world with extensive lore. Much of the work comes from his son, Christopher Tolkien, who continued making the mythology and even the 12-volume history of Middle Earth. As a professor of English and Language, Tolkien never intended his book to be a series. *The Hobbit* was originally a stand-alone book, but audiences demanded more. As a sequel, Tolkien wrote *The Lord of The Rings*, and it was so long that it had to be split into three books. He is known for creating languages used in this fantasy world and had even created them years before publishing the book, which is something that most high fantasy books leave out due to readability.

Another high fantasy series that became wildly popular because of the television adaptation is *Game of Thrones*. A series based on a medieval feel of a fantasy realm includes several aspects not found in other series. Political power struggles with every country and the differences between them. While the North works to keep watch against a looming threat, places like countries in Essos struggle with the caste system and are overthrown by an heir to the royal family in Westeros. With many storylines in place, the high fantasy element goes a long way when combining all of the backstories, languages, lore, cultures and elements that make the Westeros and Essos worlds plausible.

Portal Fantasy

In *The Chronicles of Narnia*, the book starts in a historical setting, and the children are teleported through the wardrobe to the fantasy world. What happens outside of the fantasy world is non-relevant after passing through the portal. There are different politics, races, and scenery. Years pass in Narnia, and the children who had grown into adults in Narnia find themselves back in the real world without any consequence to time as they return as children once again.

In *Jumanji*, Alan gets sucked up into the fantasy world of Jumanji. He had been missing for years, and when he returns to the real world, he is an adult. The book focuses on a fantasy element of the portal to the world of Jumanji, which also becomes part of the primary world. In this story, the board game is the portal. In the newer movie adaptation of Jumanji changes the portal from a board game to a video game.

In *The Wonderful Wizard of Oz*, Dorothy gets sucked up into a tornado in Kansas and is teleported to a foreign land. Dorothy is joined by companions to get to the great wizard who can help her get home. In this book, it turns out that Dorothy was dreaming the entire time. In *Alice in Wonderland*, the premise is similar to that of Alice falling through a hole into a fantasy realm full of friends and enemies. Like Dorothy, Alice is also in a dream world.

Anthropomorphic Fantasy

Anthropomorphic fantasies are not as common in novels as they are in children's stories. When talking animals are presented to a reader, usually they are fun and cute, which is why children's books are drawn to talking animals as opposed to adult books. In most cases, talking animals in novels represent an issue that may be easier to digest in a new way using animals. Like humans, animals have different species (races), languages, territories, and cultures.

One of the most famous novels using talking animals is George Orwell's *Animal Farm*. Orwell paints a picture of classes and revolution as farm animals take over a farm after driving out the farmer. *Animal Farm* represents the Russian Revolution along with Stalinism, portrayed by farm animals and the infamous pigs who are in charge of the farm.

Brian Jacques is known for creating the *Redwall* series featuring talking rodents, among other common animals. There are 22 books in the series, making it quite a feat for an anthropomorphic series. The different animals is either "good" or "evil," and the various species of animals are similar to comparing races. The social systems of different animals are also set in place.

Paranormal Fantasy

From Bram Stoker's *Dracula* and Anne Rice's *Interview with the Vampire* to more recent paranormal fantasy books such as *Dresden Files* and *Mortal Instruments*, paranormal novels turned into movies are quite common.

Zombies, although most may seem cliche, also can feature creative differences in novels. Perhaps the origin and how one turns into a zombie may differ from other previous versions.

Specific paranormal characters were always invented by someone, a creative author. Without Bran Stroker, we wouldn't have a Dracula or Van Helsing. Without Mary Shelley, no Dr. Frankenstein and his monster. They had left such an impression that these novel characters had turned even more into our cultural lore to where paranormal characters have become somewhat like our modern Greek gods in mythology.

Not all great paranormal ideas come from only imagination, some are based on historical characters or events. Dracula is most famously inspired by Vlad the Impaler and zombies are inspired by folklore and voodoo.

In general, a paranormal fantasy is a first-world fantasy where the supernatural occurs in the real world.

The *Twilight* series has made an impression on vampire novels turned movies. Although the general consensus is that all vampires are evil and turn to ashes in the sunlight, Stephenie Meyer has bent the rules to what a vampire is. She created a world where good and bad vampires are at war and how they sparkle in the sunlight. The *Twilight* series was so popular that even the question "Team Jake or Edward?" can be referenced years after its release.

Historical Fantasy

Unlike historical fiction, historical fantasy combines magic and fantasy elements into a historic-based setting. While fantasy may be complex regarding worldbuilding, a fair amount of research must still be done to write in a historical environment where actual events and people affect the story.

A popular book series turned television is the *Outlander* series by Diana Gabaldon. This historical fantasy combines post-WWII and 18th-century Scotland, employing magic time travel. The scenes and details are mostly historically accurate as the novels tie into historical events. After moving to Colonial America in later books, many topics, such as the redcoats, natives, customs, and places, have historical accuracy. Diana Gabaldon added events and places to her historically accurate books due to her extensive research of historical accounts.

Sometimes, historical accuracy has a prominent place in books. In *Outlander*, Claire, a nurse in WWII, makes penicillin and a hypodermic needle to save people's lives in the times of colonial America. She is concerned that, historically, Alexander Fleming invented penicillin in 1927, and she may change the course of history.

Another example is Claire knowing that Benedict Arnold, another historical figure, will be a traitor. She knows that many people will die, but her concern is for the outcome of the Revolutionary War changing if she alters the course of history.

Other books may have fewer historical events and people intertwined in the story, but for historical buffs, accuracy and relevancy is a huge plus.

Remember: A historical fantasy should have some historical accuracy with an element of fantasy such as magic.

Mythological Fantasy

Mythology in every culture starts by **explaining the unknown**. The Norse origin of the world came from an ice giant and a fire giant. The reason why the seasons change is that Hades kidnapped Persephone. The Giants Causeway in Ireland and Scotland was created by two rival giants who wanted a boxing match.

The stories in mythology were extensive as family trees, natural events, and heroes with villains came to rise. Written by several authors such as Euripedes, Heroditus, and Homer, Greek mythology remains well known and has several adaptations. This may be because Greek mythology is quite extensive. Therefore, it's easier to build a story around Greek characters and personality types.

Norse mythology is also a big player in mythological fantasy. Norse mythology has become even more popular with the rise of the Marvel universe featuring Thor and Loki.

Other mythological origins include Anubis and Ra from Egypt, Anansi from Africa, Krishna and Vishnu from India, and Maui and Pele from Polynesia.

A well-known series in mythological fantasy is *Percy Jackson and the Olympians*, written by Rick Riordan. Set in the modern day, Percy finds out that he is the son of Poseidon and must go through trials to save the world from the Titans. The personalities and roles that the mythological characters play stay true to the stories of ancient Greece.

Neil Gaiman has also taken to mythology roots for his novels and short stories in *American Gods*. Gaiman has blended a mixture of different mythological stories into one using Greek, Norse, Egyptian, and other origins. Other works from Neil Gaiman that are mythology-inspired include *The Sandman*, *Anansi Boys*, *Unnatural Creatures*, and *Norse Mythology*.

Science Fantasy

Like science fiction, many of these books are written in a future setting and rely on technology. Unlike science fiction, the technology is blended with some fantasy elements.

A *Wrinkle in Time* by Madeline L'Engle combines the science of a tesseract with a splash of magic. A tesseract in the novel is a way to travel through space and time. In the *Marvel* universe, the tesseract holds one of the sought-after infinity stones. In geometry, a tesseract is a four-dimensional cube which is a symbol for the fourth dimension.

Artemis Fowl, on the other hand, uses a world with rampant magic, fairies in particular, who have access to high-tech.

The Iris-cam is used as a camera hidden inside a contact lens.

The camfoil imitates an invisibility cloak by reflecting light and can be damaged in water due to circuitry.

The onmitool is a device that can pick most locks.

Mind-wipe uses technology to wipe certain memories.

The Bio-bomb is a bomb that is missile-guided and uses a radioactive element not known to man yet.

Magical Realism

Magical realism is similar to that of a low fantasy or first-world fantasy because it is written as if the setting occurs in our world. The big difference is that in first-world fantasy, magic is hidden away or a secret, while magical realism embraces magic in the real world.

The lines between realism and fantasy then get blurred, creating a unique world where magic is now a norm. Either magical elements can be realized, or they are so routine that it doesn't seem to be anything worth mentioning. The author usually leaves out magical elements to create the understanding that magical features are standard in the setting.

There are a few elements that make up magical realism, as it may differ from other forms of fantasy.

Realistic Setting

The setting is based on a realistic world.

Contains Fantasy Elements

Although fantasy elements are not a real-world event, in this instance, it is. Not only are there light fantasy elements, but people don't question them. They just "are".

Authorial Reticence

A term used when authors deliberately leave things out. In the case of magical realism, the author does not explain "how or why". They would write the book as if the fantasy elements were logical and expected.

Some more elements that are found in magical realism are symbolism, folklore, and emotions

Like Water for Chocolate by Laura Esquivel is a novel about a young woman named Tita whose intense emotions affect the food that she cooks and feeds to her customers. The people who eat her food are affected by the same type of emotions that Tita feels.

In *Kiki's Delivery Service* by Eiko Kodono and later adapted into a *Studio Ghibli* Film, tells of a girl who leaves home for her witch training. Kiki creates her own delivery service by delivering packages by flying on her broom. Throughout the story, witches are a known part of society, yet different people react in a variety of ways when seeing that she's a witch.

Alerian Academy

Worldbuilding

Worldbuilding is precisely what it sounds like, and for some, it may be the biggest challenge when writing fantasy, especially for high fantasy.

Worldbuilding involves several different elements that should be inserted into a novel so that the reader can fully immerse themselves in the world.

Instead of thinking about the culture of society, break down the elements of what makes a culture so you can be precise on how you can define culture in your novel.

With every part of Worldbuilding, one should always ask how the world affects the story, or even how the story affects the world. With every new world, details must be abundant for the reader to visualize something new that was created by the authors imagination.

There must also be degrees of how different and similar a fantasy world is compared to our own world.

GEOGRAPHY

Decide on if you want to make a whole world or stick to just a region. Geography includes several things: landforms, countries, cities, regions, continents, and even planets.

Are there significant locations in the world?

What are the names and basic layouts of the cities and regions?

What are the differences between these places, and how does it affect the story?

Does the geography cause obstacles?

What are the different types of flora and fauna?

What natural resources are beneficial to society?

Politics

Politics can become tricky (similarly in real life). Although you may build your own government system, you can always use real governments as an inspiration.

What kind of government system does your world have?

Are the people happy with the leadership?

How does the government change from place to place?

Do you have royalty or elected officials?

Are there any notable laws in society and how does it affect society?

SOCIETAL NORMS

Societal norms are usually informal rules that define acceptable and appropriate actions within a group of people or community. This affects standard human behavior.

How are people required to act in public?

What would happen if people don't act "normally"?

What is considered polite, and what is rude?

Are societal norms changing?

Alerian Academy

RELIGION

From the beginning of established societies, people have had different religions and beliefs that have intertwined into their culture.

What kind of religions are there in society?

What are the traditions that religion has influenced?

Are there any hostilities because of religion?

Are there major and minor religions? If so, how do they differ?

SCIENCE AND TECHNOLOGY

Science and technology in the modern day are usually marked by time and eras. We typically use terms like Industrial Era, Stone Age, and Digital Revolution. Although this is relatively true of developed countries, there are still places around the world who do not have the use of technology.

What kind of technology is used?

What kind of technology is being developed?

Is everywhere in the world at the same level scientifically?

Is there valuable technology that is pivotal in the novel?

ECONOMICS

Economics can have a great impact on how a society runs. Think of consumption, production, and trade.

What are the units of currency?

Does their society rely on trade?

How primitive or advanced are the goods and services?

What are the differences between elites and the impoverished?

What are budgets, taxes, and public investment like?

CLIMATE

Decide if you want a solar system similar to ours. We know that seasons and weather differ because of elements such as the Earth's tilt and the sun.

Do the climates vary from region to region?

How do the weather and climate affect the people in your story?

Art

Like technology, art, including music, has changed and has had various names throughout history, specifically Medieval, Renaissance, and Baroque. Unlike technology, types of art do not become obsolete.

What is viewed as art?

What kind of music and instruments are available?

How important is art to society?

How are artistic forms used in things such as architecture or human appearance?

History

History plays a role in many different ways, such as politics, borders, attitudes, traditions, religions, and much more.

What are past events that were important to society?

How does the history of region affect society today?

Are there any historical conflicts that affect behavior and attitudes in the present?

Are there any traditions or holidays due to historical events?

People

Like in our world, people are all different. Genetics and regional differences play an essential part in the differences of people.

How are the people the same or different depending on their location?

Are there different races?

How different do the people act depending on where they are from?

Is there any racism?

What is the population like?

What are the different classes, and how do they differ?

What kind of jobs do people have?

Magic

Magic is a big part of fantasy literature, but not all magic is the same, and the differences in magic can be tremendous.

What kind of magic is used?

Is magic explained or normal?

Is there a root to magic, such as genetics or drugs?

Who can wield magic?

What is the general attitude of people using magic?

What is the history or cultural significance of magic?

Is there good and bad magic?

Myths, Legends, Mythology

Although not really touched in most fiction genres, myths and legends can be a significant part of a fantasy world.

Are the myths and legends similar to that of the real world?

Are there customs that have been affected by mythology?

How important is mythology in their culture?

Language

Language is hard to construct and can be a time-sucker for worldbuilding. J.R.R. Tolkien is noted for having a wildly intensive made-up vocabulary for *The Lord of Rings*. Orwell used the term doublespeak, which is a play on words in the English language.

Do different regions speak different languages?

How does the language affect the names of places and people?

Has the language changed over time?

"After a while, the characters I'm writing begin to feel real to me. That's when I know I'm heading in the right direction."

Alice Hoffman

Characters

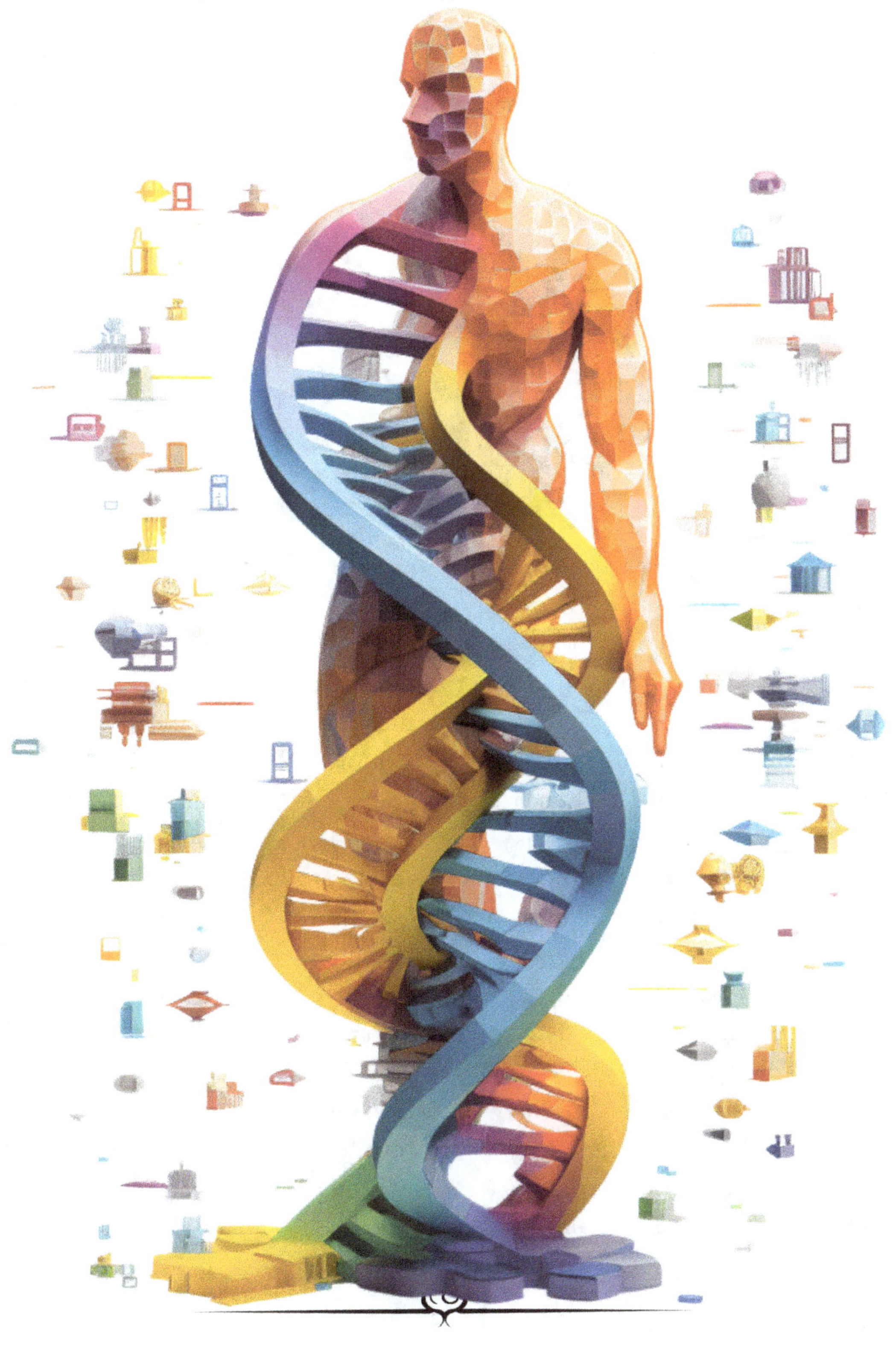

Character Appearance

Since most novels don't include pictures, it's up to the writer to tell us what characters look like. The description of a character is generally mentioned when they are first introduced. This gives the reader a vague image of what they look like before continuing on, so they can imagine them in the story. More details can be added on later down the road, but they must be consistent.

Think of this visual project as someone describing a criminal to a forensic sketch artist. Remember that visual descriptions are not meant to offend but to help the reader visualize the character.

ailing
alluring
athletic
atrophied
average
awkward
barrel-chested
battered
big-boned
bloated
bony
boyish
brittle
broad
built
bulky
bullish
burly
busty
carved
chiseled
chubby
chunky
clumsy
colossal
crippled
curvy

decomposed
decrepit
deformed
dwarfish
effeminate
familiar
feeble
feminine
formidable
fragile
frail
gangly
gargantuan
gaunt
gigantic
girlish
graceful
hairless
hairy

handsome
hardy
heavy-set
hefty
hideous
huge
hunched
hunky
hunky
husky
immense
imposing
lanky
lean
leathery
leggy
lofty
malnourished
mammoth

masculine
meaty
misshapen
monstrous
muscular
neat
nimble
obese
perfect
petite
plump
primitive
proportional
puny
rectangular
revolting
rickety
rigid
robust

round
rugged
sculpted
seductive
sensuous
sexy
shaggy
shapely
short
shredded
shrimpy
skinny
skrawny
sleek
slender
slim
slinky
slouched
squat

stacked
stately
stiff
stocky
stunning
stunted
sturdy
symmetrical
tall
toned
top-heavy
towering
trim
unclad
underdeveloped
undersized
unwashed
voluptuous
weak
whopping
wide
wimpy
wiry
withered
wrinkled
young
youthful

Tone and Color

Tone and colors give the reader detail about much more than the hue of their skin. The reader may pick up on hints on race, emotion, and even creature.

Bronze sounds like someone who is out in the sun a lot or has smooth skin.

Blushing points toward someone who may be embarrassed.

Bloodless and pale may hint towards a vampire.

The colors can also be used for various body parts such as yellowed teeth and a sunburnt nose.

alabaster	brown	creamy	ivory	rosy
albino	burnt	dark	jaundiced	ruddy
almond	butterscotch	ebony	milky	sandy
amber	buttery	espresso	mottled	sooty
apricot	caramel	fair	olive	spotted
ashen	chalky	fiery	painted	sunburnt
beige	charcoal	flushed	pale	tan
black	chestnut	freckled	pasty	tarnished
blanched	chocolate	ghostly	peach	vanilla
bloodless	coffee	ginger	pearly	washed-out
blue-tinged	colorless	golden	pink	waxen
blushing	copper	gray	porcelain	white
bronze	coral	green	red	yellowed

Complexion and Skin

acned	fine	glowing	moist	slimy	toasty
aged	firm	gnarled	musky	smooth	touchable
aromatic	flaky	goosebumps	old	soft	translucent
baby-soft	flappy	greasy	oozing	sparkling	transparent
blemished	flawed	grimy	paper-thin	speckled	unblemished
blistered	flawless	grubby	papery	splotchy	uneven
blotchy	fleshy	hairless	patchy	spongy	veined
bristly	fragrant	hairy	peeling	springy	velvet
bumpy	fresh	inflamed	perfumed	sticky	warm
burnt	frigid	leathery	pierced	streaked	weathered
caked	frostbitten	loose	pillowy	supple	wet
calloused	frozen	luminescent	pimply	sweaty	withered
chapped	furry	lumpy	puffy	swollen	wizened
chilled	fuzzy	lusterless	pure	tattooed	worn
clammy	gleaming	lustrous	radiant	thick	wrinkly
clawed	glistening	matte	sleek	tight	youthful
clean-shaven	glossy	mature	slick	tingling	rashy
clean					raw
coarse					reptilian
cool					rough
cratered					rough
damaged					scabby
delicate					scaled
dewy					scarred
dimpled					scented
dirty					scrubbed
droopy					sensitive
dry					sheer
dull					shimmering
elastic					shiny
feverish					silky

Eyes and Expression

"He has kind eyes."

Eyes are supposed to be the windows to the soul as they say. In writing, eyes are perceived as showing expression and even personality.

There is much more we can say by their eyes other than shape or color.

almond	alert	dancing	glistening	old	stormy
amber	angry	dark	glittering	oval	sultry
amethyst	animated	dead	glowing	passionate	teary
aquamarine	anxious	deep	goopy	peaceful	teasing
ash	approving	demonic	gorgeous	penetrating	telling
black	beady	disapproving	gripping	perceptive	tender
bloodshot	beckoning	discerning	happy	piercing	timid
blue	big	dramatic	hard	playful	tiny
brown	bitter	drowsy	haunting	pleasant	tired
cats eye	blank	drunk	hopeful	praising	treacherous
chestnut	blazing	dull	hungry	pure	trusting
electric blue	blinking	eager	icy	radiant	twinkling
emerald	blurry	earnest	innocent	reserved	understanding
flecked	bright	encouraging	intelligent	riveting	uneven
forest green	bug-eyed	evasive	intense	round	unkind
graphite	bulging	expressive	inviting	sad	vacant
green	burning	fierce	joyful	scary	vibrant
grey	calm	fiery	kind	serious	vivid
gunmetal	caring	flashing	laughing	sharp	warm
hazel	cautious	flat	lazy	shifty	watery
honey	cheerful	flickering	lifeless	shining	welcoming
indigo	childlike	foreboding	longing	shrewd	wide
jade	chilly	frightened	loving	sincere	wide-set
lavender	clear	frigid	luminous	slanted	wild
sapphire	close-set	frozen	lustful	sleepy	willing
sea green	cold	full	mean	small	wise
specked	comforting	generous	misty	sparkling	young
topaz	commanding	glassy	mocking	spiteful	
	crazy	gleaming	mournful	steady	
	crusty	glinting	mysterious	still	

Describing Figures

Simile: Compares two things with the words like or as.

Her hair was like golden strands weaving together in perfect unison.

Metaphor: Directly comparing two things in a non-literal sense

Her hairs were golden strands weaving together in perfect unison.

Many times we see something that starts with "built like a...."

Built like a train, a linebacker, or an action figure.

These similes and metaphors are loosely based on what you compare them to. Obviously, someone is not built like a train (that would be scary), but someone could literally be built like a linebacker (because they are real people)

The object of metaphors is to **describe in a better visual sense or even to over-exaggerate**.

Another way to describe people is to talk about something that can used in a situation.

She was so funny that nobody could stop laughing.

He was so loud that his laugh shook the walls.

He was so tall he could dunk a basketball without jumping.

Most examples of describing figures are meant to over-exaggerate.

Sometimes, you can describe figures by comparing them to inanimate objects or by adding -like after said object.

The man was barrel-chested.

Her pencil-like figure could be seen through the curtain.

His giraffe-like neck made him stand out.

Honing Descriptions

More than physical attributes

Write about how they carry themselves, their mood, how they smell, or what "vibe" they give off.

Description from another person

Everyone sees people differently. Depending on your point of view, a character could be described by how that particular character sees them.

Descriptions and personality

Descriptions could also point toward personality. A slouched man would most likely not be confident.

Don't make a list

When writing a description, don't make it into a list. Write the attributes creatively.

Missing pieces

Telling the reader what the character doesn't have has the same effect as what they do have.

Use a thesaurus

Use creative words for descriptions. Also, try to use concise words. Crazy is a little broad and overused, but deranged and maniacal may be better descriptions.

The five senses

Remember the five senses. Not only do we want to see the character, but we also want to use our senses, including the sixth sense. Are their hands soft or rough? Do they smell like sweat or fried rice?

Introductions

Although we want the reader to visualize the characters, several paragraphs of what they look like may be a bit too much to handle. It's always good to give a sample of their overall look, similar to a first impression before you get to know someone. You can add detailed descriptions throughout your story.

Too much description

Although your character may have a freckle on their shoulder in your mind, it doesn't mean that you need to share that detail. Don't describe so much that it becomes meaningless and takes away from the story.

Give them some props

A quiet girl at school with an armful of books is probably the smart one in class. If a kid is wearing a Rolex, he might be rich and act spoiled.

Interact with their surroundings

You can tell a lot about a character by how they use their surroundings, such as slamming a door, tripping over the stairs, and even bending over to pet a stray cat.

Examples of Descriptions

"Tall and rather thin but upright, the Director advanced into the room. He had a long chin and big rather prominent teeth, just covered, when he was not talking, by his full, floridly curved lips. Old, young? Thirty? Fifty? Fifty-five? It was hard to say."

-Aldous Huxley, Brave New World

"The face of Elrond was ageless, neither old nor young, though in it was written the memory of many things both glad and sorrowful. His hair was dark as the shadows of twilight, and upon it was set a circlet of silver; his eyes were grey as a clear evening, and in them was a light like the light of stars."

-J.R.R. Tolkien, Lord of the Rings: The Fellowship of the Ring

"He did not look like anything special at all."

-Johnathan Safran Foer, Everything is Illuminated

"He was most fifty, and he looked it. His hair was long and tangled and greasy, and hung down, and you could see his eyes shining through like he was behind vines. It was all black, no gray; so was his long, mixed-up whiskers. There warn't no color in his face, where his face showed; it was white; not like another man's white, but a white to make a body sick, a white to make a body's flesh crawl – a tree-toad white, a fish-belly white. As for his clothes – just rags, that was all. He had one ankle resting on t'other knee; the boot on that foot was busted, and two of his toes stuck through, and he worked them now and then. His hat was laying on the floor – an old black slouch with the top caved in, like a lid."

-Mark Twain, The Adventures of Huckleberry Finn

"I saw my Master had adorned himself in a thick tunic and beautiful dark blue doublet which I'd hardly noticed before. He wore soft sleek dark blue gloves over his hands, gloves which perfectly cleaved to his fingers, and legs were covered by thick soft cashmere stockings all the way to his beautiful pointed shoes."

-Anne Rice, The Vampire Armand

Alerian Academy

"Kinky tousled curls, only a minimum of makeup, large brown eyes behind round wire-rimmed glasses. There was a world of character in that face, more than enough to make her fascinating-looking instead of just attractive."

-Iris Johansen, The Face of Deception

"She has bright, dark eyes and satiny brown skin and stands tilted up on her toes with arms slightly extended to her sides, as if ready to take wing at the slightest sound."

-Suzanne Collins, The Hunger Games

"A giant of a man was standing in the doorway. His face was almost completely hidden by a long, shaggy mane of hair and a wild, tangled beard, but you could make out his eyes, glinting like black beetles under all the hair."

-JK Rowling, Harry Potter and the Sorcerer's Stone

"Peter was a gentle, red-haired bear of a man. Standing at six-four in his socks, he moved everywhere with a slight and nautical sway, but even though he was broad across the chest there was something centered and reassuring about him, like an old ship's mast cut from a single timber."

-Graham Joyce, Some Kind of Fairy Tale

"None of them had ever seen such...an alluring person. From the brightness on her hair, her fluorescent icy colored irises and magenta lips."

- A.L Carine, Invasion

"Pale hair fell in waves to his shoulders, framing a face mortal females considered a sensual feast. They didn't know the man was actually a devil in angel's skin. They should have, though. He practically glowed with irreverence, and there was an unholy gleam in his green eyes that proclaimed he would laugh in your face while cutting out your heart. Or laugh in your face while you cut out his heart."

- Gena Showalter, The Darkest Night

Show, Don't Tell

One of the best ways to describe a character is to show the reader who the character is, not just to describe them. Instead of accepting a description, the reader is immersed in imagination and can "see" what you describe.

When telling a story, you don't tell the audience "He has bad vision." Instead, you would write something like, "He squinted at the sign across the hall to make out the blurry words."

Instead of:

John was the tallest person in class.

Try:

The teacher asked John to get the colored paper from the top shelf, as nobody else in class was tall enough.

Instead of:

Mary was anxious.

Try:

Mary's heart beat faster with every step. Butterflies filled her stomach, and her hands were clammy. She felt as if she could hardly breathe.

Instead of:

Mom had been crying.

Try:

Mom walked out onto the patio with a cup of hot coffee in her trembling hands. Her eyes were red and swollen.

Showing, not telling, can also convey personality such as rolling of eyes, distancing oneself from a large group of people, or even a large sigh.

This concept is only for creative writing. When it comes to research papers, essays, and other forms of writing, the concept of "showing" is not used.

MBTI

Have you ever taken a personality test? Depending on the test, you could be given a set of letter (e.g. ENTJ) or perhaps a number.

Your characters will all have a set personality with variations like the Jungian archetypes mentioned before.

Below are analyses of popular (proposed) fictional characters based on Meyer Briggs.

ENFP	**ENTP**	**ENTJ**	**ENFJ**
Peter Parker	Dumbledore	President Snow	Elizabeth Bennet
Tonks	Tony Stark	Voldemort	Boromir
Mad Hatter	Willy Wonka	Irene Adler	Peeta Mellark
Ariel	Tyrion Lannister	Tywin Lannister	Charles Xavier
ESTJ	**ESFJ**	**ESFP**	**ESTP**
Prof. McGonagall	Molly Weasley	Ron Weasley	Draco Malfoy
Mycroft Holmes	Bilbo Baggins	Jaime Lannister	Indigo Montoya
Leia Organa	Cedric Diggory	Peregin Took	Gimli
Cercei Lannister	Alfred Pennyworth	Percy Jackson	Khal Drogo
ISTP	**ISFP**	**INTP**	**INTJ**
Aaragorn	Clare Fraser	Violet Baudelaire	Moriarty
John Wick	Harry Potter	Smaug	Sarumon
Black Widow	Legolas	Arthur Weasley	Hannibal Lecter
Geralt of Rivia	Eleven	Winston Smith	Severus Snape
ISTJ	**ISFJ**	**INFJ**	**INFP**
Katniss Everdeen	Samwise Gangee	Prince Caspian	Bella Swan
Jon Snow	Dr. Watson	Galadriel	Frodo
Dr. Alan Grant	Steve Rogers	Remus Lupin	Faramir
Thorin Oakenshield	Charlie Buckets	Lord Varys	Lucy Pevense

Characteristics

Although character flaws make a good story, positive attributes help the hero prevail. Positive traits also make great sidekicks, but they may also help readers empathize with the bad guy, who also can have positive traits. Different traits also give a more profound understanding to who they are, what they want, why they have that specific trait, and how it is relevant to the story. Every trait can be broken down and can be used in the story or for character development.

Take the positive trait "observant," for example. The causes can be anywhere from a fear of missing something or paranoia, which are prime examples of negative traits that contribute to a positive trait. The behavior would be modified by actions such as eavesdropping, commenting on something that has changed, or remembering important details. An observant person is more likely to be the detective in a novel. On the other hand, an unobservant person in the novel may annoy the observant character, and arguing can ensue.

Character Flaws

Characters are relatable in a variety of ways. Some of the most relatable characteristics are flaws. Perhaps the reader is a jealous person; therefore, they can relate to an action that a character in your novel does because of that jealousy.

Characters are not perfect, but remember that character flaws can shape your story and make that particular flaw useful to the character's storyline.

The interesting thing about flaws is that a lot of them are perceived differently in the readers (and other characters) eyes. For example, bluntness can be a character flaw. It may land your character in trouble or outside of a social circle, but at the same time, it may be able to help the character in some way.

There are generally three categories of character flaws.

Minor Flaw

A minor flaw is something that many readers may have in common with a character. It may cause the character to act or say something that may hint at the flaw, but it is not glaringly obvious. These are flaws that may be fixed over time.

Major Flaw

A major flaw is undeniable. It causes a certain amount of hostility or chaos. It changes parts of the story and sometimes causes the character to act irrationally. The major flaw is usually a hindrance to the character and their life, and not everyone can relate.

Fatal Flaw

This kind of flaw, as the name states, can be fatal. It brings on the downfall of the characters and can change the story dramatically. In general, it is a flaw you don't see more than once in a novel.

Common and easily noticeable flaws are physical flaws. In real life, these flaws are what we see as first impressions.

Lists of Character Flaws

The most common and easily noticeable minor flaws tend to be physical appearance. Judging a book by its cover is simple and easy in novels and in reality. In a novel, physical appearance is usually noted right away.

Chewed on fingernails	Acne	Large ears or cauliflower ears
Missing limbs or body parts	Body hair or no hair	Crooked nose
Lazy eye or cross eyed	Warts or moles	Tattoos and piercings
Overweight or underweight	Bad or missing teeth	Posture
Scars and burns	Bad hygiene or odor	Obvious plastic surgery

Some personality traits may be more neutral than positive or negative, depending on a personal definition. For example, the trait *quirky* is used to describe someone. This can either be taken positively, negatively, or neutrally. The definition can also be different depending on situation.

There are also **positive traits that can be viewed as negative just because of the character who displays that specific trait**. "Convincing" would be considered a positive trait in an instance with a coach trying to get a talented individual to play on a team, yet being convincing as a grifter would general be perceived as a bad person doing a bad thing because of the intention.

Absent-minded	Bad-tempered	Competitive	Difficult
Abusive	Belittling	Complainer	Dimwit
Addict	Bigmouth	Controlling	Dishonest
Adulterous	Bigot	Critical	Disloyal
Aimless	Blunt	Cruel	Disorderly
Anxious	Bold	Cursed	Disrespectful
Argumentative	Bully	Cusser	Disturbed
Arrogant	Callous	Deceptive	
Attached	Childish	Dependent	
Audacious	Clumsy	Deranged	

Alerian Academy

Dolt	Incompetent	Passive-Aggressive	Spoiled
Drunkard	Inconsiderate	Pathological Liar	Squander
Easily-Angered	Indecisive	Perfectionist	Squeamish
Egotistical	Indifferent	Pessimist	Steadfast
Envious	Indomitable	Pest	Storyteller
Erratic	Infamy	Phobic	Stubborn
Exploiter	Inhumane	Possessive	Superstitious
Explosive	Intolerant	Predictable	Suspicious
Fanatical	Irrational	Pretentious	Sycophant
Fickle	Judgmental	Prideful	Tactless
Fierce	Klutz	Racist	Tease
Finicky	Lazy	Rebellious	Temperamental
Fixated	Lewd	Reckless	Tenacious
Flake	Lustful	Remorseless	Theatrical
Flirty	Manipulative	Rigorous	Thoughtless
Gluttonous	Materialistic	Robin Hood	Threatening
Greedy	Meddlesome	Sadistic	Timid
Gullible	Megalomaniac	Sarcastic	Tongue-tied
Harasser	Nagging	Skeptic	Troublemaker
Humorous	Naïve	Seducer	Unethical
Humorless	Narcissistic	Self-righteous	Unforgiving
Hypocrite	Negligent	Selfish	Unfriendly
Idealist	Nervous	Senile	Unlucky
Idiotic	Nosy	Shallow	Unpredictable
Ignorant	Obsessive	Slacker	Unsupportive
Illiterate	Offensive	Smart Ass	Untrustworthy
Immature	Oppressor	Smoker	Vain
Immoral	Overambitious	Soft-hearted	Vindictive
Impatient	Overconfident	Solemn	Weak-willed
Impetuous	Overemotional	Spender	Withdrawn
Impish	Overprotective	Spineless	Workaholic
Impulsive	Paranoid	Spiteful	Zealous

Seven Deadly Sins

When books were only defined as Comedy or Tragedy, Dante Alighieri wrote a trilogy called **The Divine Comedy**. It is divided into three parts: **Inferno**, **Purgatorio**, and **Paradiso**.

Although most people haven't read the entirety of *The Divine Comedy*, many people are aware of the message of the seven deadly sins that were the philosophical statements of Dante. Originally written as nine sins, adaptations and translations have left us with the modern seven deadly sins.

Lust

Intense longing, adultery, bestiality, and sexual acts.

Could also mean a desire for worldly things, such as money or power.

Wrath

Anger, rage, and hatred that is uncontrollable. Anger is human nature, but when it is directed towards an innocent person or when there are feelings of vengeance involved, it becomes a deadly sin.

Glutton

Overindulgence and over-consumption.

Could also be attributes to eating too expensive or eagerly, as well as glutton for things that are not food.

Sloth

Without care of mental, spiritual, and physical states. It includes absence of interest and laziness

Greed

A strong desire to acquire or possess more than one needs, usually leaving less for others. Worldly and materialistic as well as non tangible greed.

Envy

An insatiable coveting of the traits or possessions of someone else. Envy is the cause of actions such as lowering another's reputation, joy at another's misfortune, and grief at another's prosperity.

Pride

The excessive views of oneself, could also be called vanity. Religious views also attribute the fact of denouncing what God has provided for you because of internal pride.

The seven deadly sins inspire a large amount of popular culture, From *Willy Wonka* to *Full Metal Alchemist*, the use of basic character flaws provides great stories and character challenges.

Character Positives

Positive traits are something to be proud of. They help us root for the good guy and confuse us when it comes to the bad guy. They give readers hope, a sense of morality, and values.

If you put the word "over" before many positive traits, they may actually become negative traits. For example, "confident" is a positive trait. To be confident, you may be able to overcome hardships, make tough decisions on the spot, and give great speeches. Once you become too confident or overconfident, it can turn into a character flaw.

Accurate	Creative	Helpful	Meticulous	Proactive	Sentimental
Adaptable	Curious	Honest	Modern	Productive	Simple
Adventurous	Decisive	Honorable	Modest	Professional	Sophisticated
Affectionate	Dependable	Hospitable	Neat	Proficient	Spiritual
Alert	Diplomatic	Humble	Nurturing	Prompt	Spontaneous
Ambitious	Disciplined	Idealistic	Obedient	Proper	Spunky
Analytical	Discreet	Imaginative	Objective	Protective	Studious
Appreciative	Easygoing	Independent	Observant	Punctual	Suave
Artistic	Efficient	Individualistic	Open-Minded	Purposeful	Supportive
Attentive	Empathetic	Industrious	Optimistic	Quirky	Talented
Bold	Enthusiastic	Innocent	Organized	Realistic	Thoughtful
Calm	Ethical	Inspirational	Passionate	Reasonable	Thrifty
Cautious	Fetching	Intelligent	Patient	Relaxed	Tolerant
Centered	Flamboyant	Interesting	Patriotic	Resourceful	Traditional
Charming	Focused	Inventive	Pensive	Respectful	Trusting
Clean	Forgiving	Just	Perceptive	Responsible	Trustworthy
Clever	Frank	Kind	Persistent	Romantic	Uninhibited
Confident	Friendly	Likable	Persuasive	Self-Confident	Unselfish
Consistent	Funny	Logical	Philosophical	Self-Disciplined	Warm
Constructive	Generous	Loyal	Playful	Self-Reliant	Whimsical
Convincing	Gentle	Mature	Polite	Sensible	Wholesome
Courageous	Grateful	Merciful	Positive	Sensual	Wise
Courteous	Happy	Methodical	Private	Sentimental	Witty

Introverted and Extroverted

The most significant, most common indicator of a character's personality is how they interact with the people around them. As previously mentioned with personality types (Myers-Briggs), the E and the I reflect whether or not the specific person is extroverted or introverted. While neither is good or bad, too much of either may be a problem in a character's storyline.

Many people can identify as an amnivert or omnivert.

Amnivert: identify as both introverted and extroverted in a specific situation. This can be based on comfort level, situation, and caution.

Omnivert: identify as both introverted and extroverted but are sometimes extreme and uncontrolled.

Remember that introversion and extroversion isn't all about how social someone is, but rather **how an individual reacts in a social situation**.

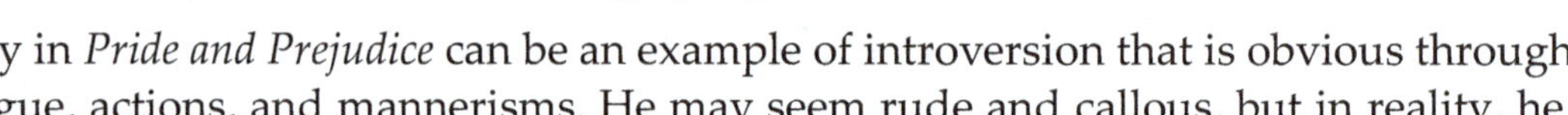

Mr. Darcy in *Pride and Prejudice* can be an example of introversion that is obvious through his dialogue, actions, and mannerisms. He may seem rude and callous, but in reality, he just doesn't want to be around people and acts accordingly.

On the other hand, Lydia Bennet is known for being immature and impulsive. She is viewed as a poor planner and emotional. She has great self-confidence and would throw herself in any social situation for fun.

In *The Hunger Games*, Katniss Everdeen is written as an introvert. She keeps to herself and can spend hours in the woods hunting. Peeta Mellark is the opposite. He can talk to people, and he can put on a show. He is described as charming and likable.

Putting introverts together with extroverts in a social or pressing situation can make a book more interesting. These manufactured situations add character depth if you carefully document their interactions.

Emotions

Emotions come in all shapes and forms. Language is tricky because **some words show a very specific type or degree of emotion.** *Angry* is a broad emotion, but narrowing it down to *furious* can be easily understood and direct. Below are many examples of words to use in a novel to convey specific emotions.

Sad	Anger	Joy	Fear	Love
agony	aggravated	amused	alarmed	affectionate
alienated	agitated	awe	anxious	adore
anguish	annoyed	blissful	apprehensive	affectionate
defeated	bitterness	cheerful	distressed	aroused
depressed	contempt	content	dreadful	attracted
despair	disgusted	delighted	fearful	caring
disappointed	dislike	eager	frightened	compassionate
dismayed	envious	ecstatic	horrified	desire
displeasure	exasperated	elated	hysterical	fond
gloomy	ferocity	enjoyed	mortified	infatuation
glumness	frustrated	enthralled	nervous	liking
grief	fury	enthusiastic	panicked	lustful
guilty	hate	excited	scared	longing
hopeless	hostility	exhilarated	shocked	passionate
hurting	irritation	euphoric	tense	sentimental
insecure	grouchy	glad	terrified	tender
isolated	grumpy	glee	uneasy	
lonely	jealous	happy	worried	
melancholy	loathing	hopeful		
miserable	mad	jolly		
neglected	outrage	pleasureful	embarrassed	surprised
regretful	rage	optimistic	humiliated	proud
rejected	repulsive	proud	insulted	triumphant
remorseful	resentment	relief	amazed	nauseated
shameful	scorned	satisfied	tired	offended
sorrowful	spiteful	thrilled	astonished	horrified
suffering	vengeful	triumphant	unnerved	thankful
unhappy	wrath		serene	smug
woeful				

Plutchik's Wheel

Psychiatrist Robert Plutchik created a theoretical cone of emotions that could be laid out flat as a 2D model. It classifies emotions and responses using a psycho-evolutionary approach. He used eight primary emotions: anger, fear, sadness, disgust, surprise, anticipation, trust, and joy.

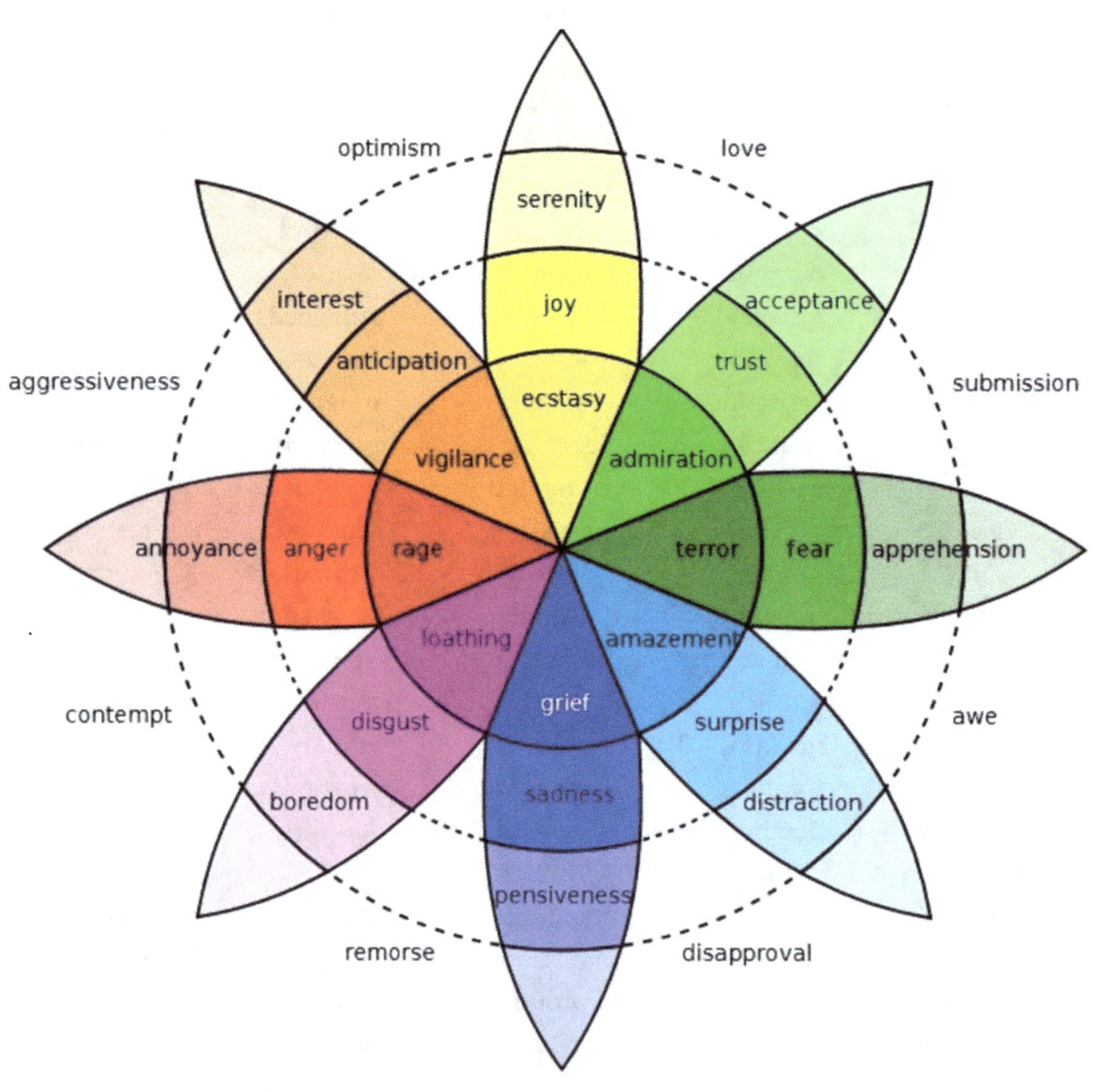

Character Expansion

MOTIVE

Although motive may sound like an ill-intentioned word thrown around in a courtroom, characters always have a reason when doing something.

REPUTATION

A character's reputation can either be good or bad. If a hacker is hired for an important job, he will have a reputation among his prospective employers.

HABITS AND PATTERNS

A character's habits can tell a lot about them. A woman who spends much time preparing in the morning may lack confidence or be egotistic. A habit of looking at one's phone for the time may indicate that they dislike being late.

TASTES AND PREFERENCES

Preferences usually do not change a story dramatically, but they do change the perception of the character actions.

SELF AND PERSONA

Many people have a self (the face to keep to themselves) and a persona (the face to show the world). Readers must be able to distinguish between the two.

TALENTS AND ABILITIES

Think of someone like Robert Langdon in *The Da Vinci Code*. Not only is he an intelligent professor, but he has the knowledge and expertise to solve mysteries because of his ability to understand and decipher symbols.

STEREOTYPES

A well-known stereotype in the comic world would be Bruce Wayne. Living out a rich playboy life in the daytime is a cover for Batman, and people may never put them both together because of stereotyping.

TENSION

Books that have strong emotions will also have tension. Like viewing tension across a room, the reader should be able to feel the tension by reading dialogue and actions.

Cultural SIGNIFICANCE

Make sure your character fits in a cultural frame. This includes names, habits, and customs. A quinceanera might be something on a young girl's mind if she is Mexican.

EMOTIONAL STAKES

Conflict and resolutions usually come with emotional stakes. Fears, suffering, sacrifice, and much more can affect the story and the outcome of the protagonist.

Deviant Behavior

Deviance describes actions that go against what is expected in society. The opposite of deviance is **conformity**.

Formal deviance includes crimes and violations of laws.

Informal deviance refers to violations of relaxed social norms, like talking loudly or picking one's nose.

Historical deviance: deviance to particular norms that have changed over time. Something that was viewed as acceptable back then, but is not acceptable now. Smoking, historically, was something trendy. Now, it's seen as dangerous or disgusting.

Cultural deviance: different things are seen as deviant depending on the culture. In America, people are expected to tip for services. In many other countries, tips are nonexistent.

Situational deviance: the same action can be deemed as conformist in one situation and deviant in another. Wearing a bikini is normal for women and deviant for men. Wearing a bikini at the beach is normal, but wearing one at school would be deviant.

Any character in a novel can have deviant behavior. Most likely, a villain will have formal deviant behavior, but heroes can have them as well.

Think of anti-heroes. What makes them less than perfect is most likely the abundance of deviance. Even Ariel from *The Little Mermaid* was deviant.

We know villains usually have formal deviance, but what if they had no informal deviance? They looked good, didn't raise red flags, were courteous and polite, and seemed to follow the rules. People don't see them as the villain, which makes them even more dangerous.

Now think of a hero, such as *Sherlock Holmes*, who is riddled with informal deviance (sometimes formal) to do his job. On the other hand, *James Bond*, who looks perfect socially, can have no informal deviance, yet has to use formal deviance to do his job.

Alerian Academy

In addition to show not tell, dialogue is essential when trying to show you what kind of person a character is. Rarely will an author list out characteristics of a certain character.

The reader's opinion of a character is formed by not only the author's description but also from their actions and what they say.

Character dialogue can indicate growth in self.

Readers can easily assess relationships as the novel progresses.

Readers are able to guess characters' thoughts without their POV.

Readers can discern personality through dialogue.

In addition to character archetypes, Carl Jung mapped out what makes up someone's personality and archetype. Below is a diagram of Carl Jung's perception of what made up human personality and behavior.

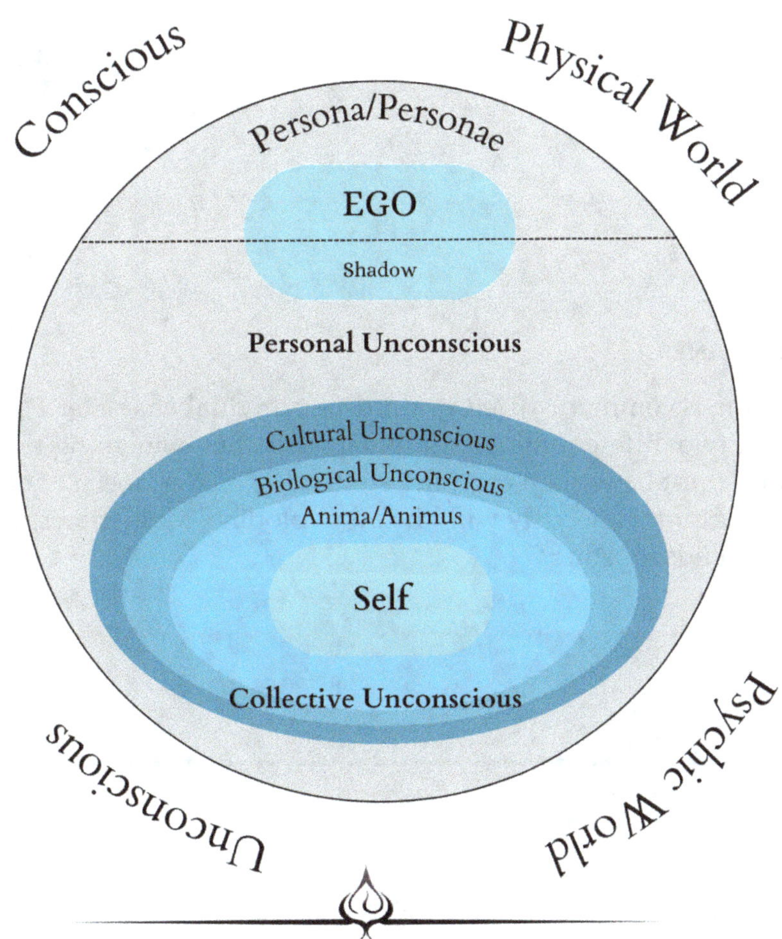

Plotlines

Sometimes, having one plot with an A to Z beeline is boring. Perhaps there's more you want to share than just one story. This can easily be remedied in a few ways, but authors must carefully master the balancing act of multiple plots.

SUBPLOTS

Subplots are small stories that deviate from the main story. Carefully include important details in these subplots. Subplots are known for adding character details and intensifying the "action". They can also start a chain reaction that spills into the main plot. Subplots can also assist in revealing something important the main character is unaware of, but the reader should be informed of it.

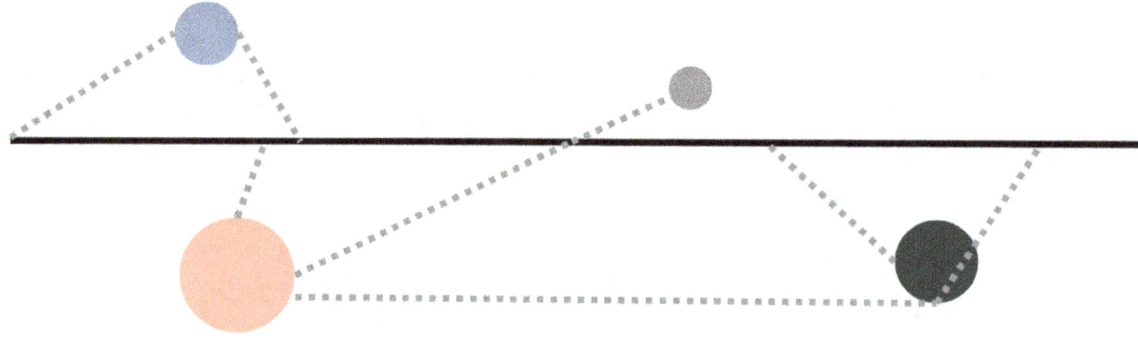

PARALLEL PLOTLINES

A parallel plotline is commonly used in third-person dual character POV. Think of two characters doing two different things simultaneously, but something ties them together. Parallel plotlines must be written carefully so that the reader doesn't get confused about what is happening simultaneously with the other plotline. Many times, a parallel plotline starts together or ends together.

Alerian Academy

WOVEN PLOTS

Like parallel plotlines, woven or braided plots involve different people at the same time. Perhaps you want to take it a little further than two people and have them connect at various points. Movies have popularized this type of plotline and it may be easier to follow in movies because of the visualization of characters. Like *A Song of Ice and Fire* (*Game of Thrones*), several people have their own stories and plotlines, but one or different features connect them.

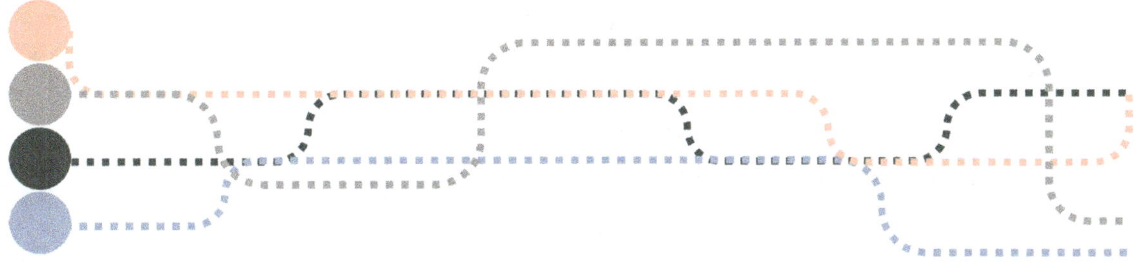

FLASHBACKS

Flashbacks are great when they provide context to the story. Want to know why a character has a trigger? Traumatic flashback. Why did the character act a certain way? Flashback. Why do they want to visit France so much? Flashback. Flashbacks are a great way to stay true to the "show, don't tell" idea where the character shouldn't explain something that happened in the past but for the reader to experience the past.

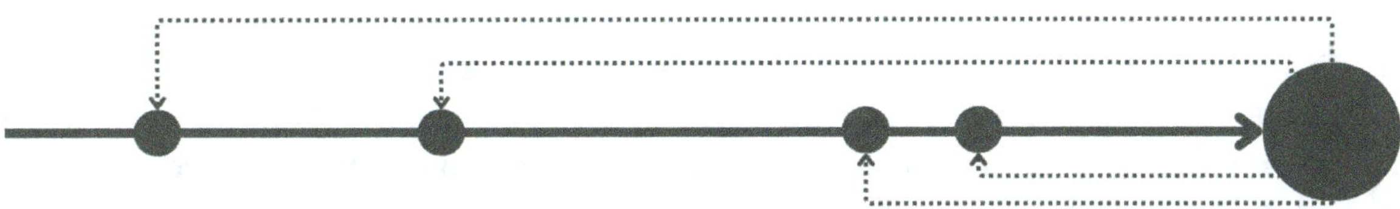

EPISODIC PLOTS

An episodic plot structure is a story divided into distinct episodes or self-contained segments, each with its own events, conflicts, and resolutions. Usually, each episode contributes to the larger narrative while having its own unique elements. Think of it like a TV show with episodes.

The **Point of View** for a novel is generally written in first person or third person. The type of POV depends on the perspective that the writer uses. The easiest way to discern POV is by the use of different pronouns.

First person: I walked to the house.

Second person: You walked to the house.

Third person: He walked to the house.

(Second person is generally used in things like instruction manuals)

Think of who you want to tell the story, as there are pros and cons in any point of view you choose.

FIRST-PERSON

Narrating from the writer's/protagonist's eyes, this can be in-depth feeling-wise, making the story realistic and relatable. One drawback is that you cannot write what any other characters are feeling or thinking.

THIRD-PERSON NARRATOS

The narrator knows everyone's actions; however, the reader may not be able to connect as well, depending on how you write the thoughts of the characters.

THIRD-PERSON CHARACTER

Like the first person, you can deep dive into one of your characters. You can easily input thoughts, feelings, and the subconscious. Unlike the narrator, however, you may be unable to "see" anything other than what happens to that character. If your character is about to kick in a door, they do not know who's waiting for them on the opposite side because they can't see it.

THIRD-PERSON DUAL CHARACTER

Some books may use two character viewpoints. This can be a hero and villain or two lovers. This lets you see how both of them feel and how they interact. You can also write two events that happened at the same time from both of their perspectives. Finding the pacing and flow to this style may be tricky.

THIRD-PERSON MULTI-CHRACTER

Perhaps you want to follow around ten different characters. This is tricky, but is excellent for getting into the minds of the different characters and creating unique personalities. Set up multiple viewpoints immediately so you don't confuse the reader later in the book. Viewpoints can change with every chapter.

"Your intuition knows what to write, so get out of the way."

Ray Bradbury

"What monster sleeps in the deep of your story? You need a monster. Without a monster there is no story."

Billy Marshall

"Read, read, read. Read everything--trash, classics, good and bad, and see how they do it. Just like a carpenter who works as an apprentice and studies the master. Read! You'll absorb it. Then write. If it's good, you'll find out. If it's not, throw it out of the window."

William Faulkner

"Either write something worth reading or do something worth writing."

Benjamin Franklin

"You can't wait for inspiration. You have to go after it with a club."

Jack London

"Good novels are not written by orthodoxy-sniffers, nor by people who are conscience-stricken about their own orthodoxy. Good novels are written by people who are not frightened."

George Orwell

"You have to write the book that wants to be written. And if the book will be too difficult for grown-ups, then you write it for children."

Madeleine L'Engle

"If there's a book that you want to read, but it hasn't been written yet, then you must write it."

Toni Morrison

"If you have any young friends who aspire to become writers, the second greatest favor you can do them is to present them with copies of The Elements of Style. The first greatest, of course, is to shoot them now, while they're happy."

Dorothy Parker

Editing

and Grammar

Grammar Rules?

Grammar may seem like an easy task: Follow the rules.

Unfortunately (or fortunately), writing a novel is not always cut and dry.

There are numerous times when you'll be reading a book and notice that the sentence that you may have just read isn't technically a complete sentence. Perhaps you've noticed a few run-on sentences, but they were filled with visual details that helped elevate the paragraph.

Grammar is important, but not all the rules or recommendations apply to novel writing.

She stared at the picture.

"Brian."

In this example, "Brian" would not be considered a complete sentence. This is an example of breaking a grammatical rule in favor of telling the story. The girl is sad or misses Brian. It is understood. It wouldn't be as dramatic as saying, "I miss Brian."

Grammar is a part of language invented by people to make things more fluid and cohesive. Verbal language is part of society that has been formed over time. When telling a story, write it as if you are verbally telling the story. The reason for editing the book with certain grammatical rules is just for readability, not to make the book interesting.

You must first learn the rules so you that you know how to break them effectively.

Alerian Academy

Punctuation

The biggest punctuation question while writing a novel versus other forms of writing is how quotations should be punctuated.

- A standard dialogue sentence looks like this:

"Dialogue," said the character.

Periods, exclamation points, question marks, and commas fall inside the quotation marks.

- Use a comma to introduce dialogue.

He said, "The napkins are in the bag."

- When a tag follows the dialogue (said, asked, etc.), use a comma. Even though a character may have said a full sentence, use a comma when there is a tag after the dialogue. When there is no tag, end the sentence with the appropriate punctuation.

"Look at my book," she said.

"Look at my book."

- Use exclamation points or question marks with the dialogue to show emotion or a question, whether there is a tag or not.

"Look at my book!" she yelled.

"Look at my book!"

"When should I go?" he asked.

- Use a different paragraph every time the dialogue speaker changes. Keep the same paragraph if the speaker is the same.

"Gather your things," she said. "We don't want to be late."

"How long will the trip take?"

"About an hour."

- Use single quotation when using quotes within dialogue

"My mom always said 'keeping calm is a virtue' in times like this," she said.

- Use capitalization for the next sentence after a tag unless the first sentence wasn't complete and the second part is a continuation.

"He found a penny on the ground," she said. "Watch that he doesn't put it in his mouth."

"What do you mean," he said to Jenna, "by she isn't coming?"

Capitalization

Aside from the obvious capitalization of the first letter in a sentence, capitalization occurs with proper nouns. There are a few exceptions and rules to watch out for when capitalizing words.

A **common noun** is a person, place, or thing but not particular or special; they are generic nouns.

Proper nouns are nouns that are capitalized. These include names of people, places, and brand names.

Common nouns include: country, river, tower, girl

Proper nouns include: Argentina, Mississippi River, Eiffel Tower, Mary

FAMILY MEMBERS

Sometimes, we use nouns like mom or dad as a name. When we use it in that sense, the word is capitalized.

Ask Mom if she will be on time.

Can you ask your mom if she will be late?

I saw Uncle Lois at the store.

Your uncle was talking with our teacher.

TITLES

Some titles are used as names. In these instances, the title itself is not capitalized, but if the title is combined with someone's name as if it were part of their name, then it is capitalized.

I ran into Professor Jackson today.

I ran into my professor today.

SEASONS

Seasons should only be capitalized when used in a name.

Are you going to Winter Formal?

I will visit him in the winter.

DIRECTIONS

Directions are not capitalized unless used as part of the proper name or region.

He is from West Virginia.

Go past the hardware store, then turn west.

BRAND NAMES

Sometimes, a brand name turns into a **collective noun**. For example, "Kleenex" is a brand name but is commonly used to talk about facial tissues. This is easily confused for brands such as "Tupperware" instead of plastic containers or "Q-tips" instead of double-sided cotton swabs.

Brand names should be capitalized, and avoiding the brand names for collective nouns is recommended.

She needs a Kleenex.

She needs a tissue.

Although both are technically correct, the first one would refer to Kleenex, the brand, while the second sentence would refer to a generic tissue, Kleenex or not.

Don't forget these capitalizations.

- Holidays and events
- Months
- Titles - don't capitalize articles (a, an, the), conjunctions (and), or prepositions (with) unless these words begin or end the title.
- Organization names - capitalize letters of acronyms that represent organizations.
- Letter salutations and closings
- Languages and race - even dialects
- Time periods - historical eras

Compound Sentences

When it comes to sentences, writing a novel is wildly different than an essay. The extra words used to describe something make the sentence longer, creating a run-on effect for most readers. These sentences use more than one clause, or idea, per sentence, making the sentence a longer and more enticing sentence to read.

A **complex sentence** has one independent clause and at least one dependent clause.

A **compound sentence** has two or more independent clauses joined by coordinating conjunctions or a semicolon.

Each independent clause in a compound sentence could stand alone as a complete sentence because the elements are similar or equal in value.

For: indicates a reason or cause

And: connects similar ideas or adds information

Nor: joins two negative alternatives

But: contrasts or presents an alternative

Or: alternative or a choice

Yet: contrast or contradiction

So: consequence or result

She wanted to go to the concert, but she had to work.

Independent clause 1: She wanted to go to the concert.

Independent clause 2: She had to work.

In this example, both independent clauses can function as standalone sentences, but they are connected to convey a relationship between the ideas.

Compound sentences are different from a compound subject or compound predicate.

Bill and Mary went to the store. - is an example of a compound subject because it combines two subjects in the same sentence.

Bill went to the store and the park. - is an example of a compound predicate, as Bill is the subject and the park and the store are the two combined predicate.

Complex Sentences

A complex sentence consists of one independent clause (a complete sentence that can stand alone) and at least one dependent clause (a group of words that has a subject and a verb but cannot or should not stand alone as a complete sentence).

Complex sentences use subordinating conjunctions to show the relationship between one independent clause and a dependent clause based on the type of subordinating conjunction.

- Cause and Effect

because, since, as, so that

- Contrast

although, though, even though, while, whereas

- Time

when, while, before, after, since, until, as soon as, whenever

- Condition

if, unless, in case, provided that

- Compromise

although, even though, though, while

"Although it was raining, she went for a walk.

Independent clause: "*She went for a walk.*"

Dependent clause: "*Although it was raining.*"

In this example, the independent clause can stand alone as a complete sentence, but the dependent clause cannot. The dependent clause standing alone doesn't make the same amount of sense or carry the same meaning without the independent clause.

In many instances, you may find yourself writing a compound-complex sentence.

After finishing her work, Maria joined her friends for dinner, and even though she was tired, they persuaded her to stay for a movie, which turned out to be a great decision.

Independent clauses: "*Maria joined her friends for dinner*" and "*They persuaded her to stay for a movie.*"

Dependent clause: "*After finishing her work*" and "*even though she was tired*" and "*which turned out to be a great decision.*"

They Said "What?"

Dialogue can get tricky by using the word "said" too many times. Yes, the character did say it, but using words other than "said" is vital to the details and readability of the dialogue. Not only will it make your sentences dynamic, but reader tags give precise feelings to dialogue.

Pay attention to the tone of the speaker and the situation. Some words that are similar such as informed and reported still have a slight difference depending on the dialogue.

accused	barked	cheered	contended	denied	flirted
acknowledged	bawled	chimed in	continued	denounced	forgave
added	beamed	chirped	contributed	described	fretted
added	began	chorused	conversed	dictated	fumed
addressed	begged	chuckled	convinced	directed	gagged
admired	bellowed	claimed	cooed	disagreed	gasped
admitted	beseeched	clarified	corrected	disclosed	giggled
advised	bet	coached	counseled	disputed	gloated
affirmed	bickered	coaxed	countered	divulged	greeted
agreed	bleated	comforted	cried	doubted	grieved
announced	blubbered	commanded	cried out	echoed	grinned
answered	blurted	commented	cringed	empathized	griped
apologized	boasted	complained	criticized	encouraged	groaned
appealed	boomed	complimented	croaked	ended	growled
approved	bragged	conceded	crowed	enunciated	grumbled
argued	breathed	concluded	cursed	erupted	grunted
articulated	burst	concurred	dared	exasperated	guessed
asked	cackled	condemned	debated	exclaimed	gulped
asserted	cajoled	confessed	decided	explained	gurgled
assured	called	confided	declared	exploded	gushed
attested	cautioned	confirmed	defended	expressed	heaved
babbled	challenged	congratulated	deflected	faltered	hesitated
badgered	chastised	considered	deflected	finished	hinted
bantered	chattered	consoled	demanded	flattered	hissed

hollered
howled
huffed
hummed
hypothesized
imitated
imparted
implied
implored
inclined
informed
inquired
insinuated
insisted
instructed
insulted
interjected
interrupted
invited
jabbered
jeered
jested
joked
joshed
lamented
lectured
lethargically
lied
maintained
marveled
mentioned
mimicked
moaned
mocked
motioned

mourned
mouthed
mumbled
murmured
muttered
nagged
nodded
noted
notified
objected
observed
offered
ordered
panted
peeped
perplexed
persuaded
pestered
petitioned
piped
pleaded
pointed out
pondered
praised
prayed
pressed
probed
proclaimed
prodded
professed
promised
prompted
pronounced
proposed
protested

provoked
purred
put forth
put in
puzzled
quaked
quavered
queried
questioned
quipped
quizzed
quoted
raged
rambled
ranted
rasped
rattled on
read
reasoned
reassured
recalled
recited
reckoned
recounted
refused
reiterated
rejoiced
rejoined
related
remarked
remembered
reminded
repeated
replied

reported
requested
resounded
responded
restated
retaliated
retorted
revealed
rhymed
ridiculed
roared
sang
sassed
scoffed
scolded
scowled
screamed
screeched
seethed
shared
shivered
shot
shouted
shrieked
shrilled
shuddered
sighed
slurred
smiled
smirked
snapped
snarled
sneered
sneezed

snickered
sniffled
sniveled
snorted
sobbed
soothed
spat
specified
speculated
spilled
spluttered
spoke
spoke up
sputtered
squawked
squeaked
squealed
stammered
started
stated
stormed
stressed
stumbled
stuttered
suggested
supposed
surmised
swooned
swore
sympathized
taunted
teased
tempted
tested

testified
theorized
thought
threatened
thundered
told
trembled
tried
trumpeted
urged
uttered
ventured
verified
voiced
volunteered
vowed
wailed
warned
welcomed
went on
wept
wheezed
whimpered
whined
whispered
whooped
wished
wondered
worried
yakked
yapped
yawned
yelled
yelped

Tags

Adverbial tags

"I see it," she said <u>quietly</u>

Adverbial tags are generally thought to be used in "amateur" writing. Many authors will tell you to take out most adverbs as they're considered lazy ways to describe something happening. This comes hand in hand with "show, don't tell".

Other ways to use dialogue tags.

"I see it," **he said in a** hushed tone.

"I see it," **she said with** curious eyes.

"I see it," **he said with a** small smile.

97

Paragraphs

Paragraphs can be tricky as it is somewhat up to the writer's discretion on how to use them. There are only a few rules, but most are recommendations for writing and creating paragraphs.

In school, we are taught that a paragraph consists of about five sentences, and each paragraph should have a different main idea. The idea that paragraphs should have a minimum number of sentences is non-existent in novel writing.

There is a general consensus, however, of too long of a paragraph as you do not want a paragraph to last a whole page.

Start a new paragraph when:

- the scenery changes.

- the time changes or there is a gap in time

- when the speaker changes

- a flashback starts

- there is a new topic or idea that changes the focus

Camera angle effect

A scene doesn't have just one camera angle when you watch a movie. When there are two people talking to each other, usually the camera angle switches from person to person. In a group scene, many angles are taken instead of one widescreen shot. Think of your paragraphs as these camera angles.

Don't start a new paragraph for the same character in dialogue and in thoughts.

Keep a paragraph to a short sentence for dramatic effect.

Shorter paragraphs are great for action, while longer paragraphs are used for drawn-out scenes.

Paragraphs adjust the pace of the reader.

Paragraphs always use indents. This is a perfect visual tool for readers to understand the pace, who's talking, and what the main idea is.

The punctuation for dialogue may be a little counter-intuitive when it comes to paragraphs. If the dialogue for the same person continues into the next paragraph, the quotation marks are not placed at the end of the paragraph. Quotation marks should start at the beginning of the next paragraph regardless of who is speaking.

Spell Check

While there are many programs out there that check spelling, a handful also use grammar check as well. Free and paid versions exist, but it is a good investment to use a paid service.

There are some disadvantages to using a spell and grammar check. The writer must always be vigilant and not always change the flagged corrections blindly.

FALSE POSITIVES

Spelling and grammar checkers may sometimes flag correct language usage as errors or suggest unnecessary changes. Users need to evaluate suggestions to avoid introducing errors.

CONTEXTUAL UNDERSTANDING

Online tools do not always have the ability to fully understand the context of a sentence. This can result in incorrect suggestions, especially when dealing with ambiguous or complex language constructs.

LIMITED TO STANDARD GRAMMAR RULES

Grammar checkers often follow standard grammatical rules, which may not account for the nuances of creative writing, dialogue, or specific style choices. Writers may need to override suggestions to maintain their unique voice.

INABILITY TO CATCH MISUSED WORDS

Some tools may not effectively catch misused words if the error results in a correctly spelled word. For instance, confusing "there" and "their" might go unnoticed by some tools.

LACK OF STYLE GUIDANCE

Spelling and grammar checkers may not provide guidance on writing style, tone, or other subjective elements. Writers seeking more comprehensive feedback may need to consult additional resources or human editors.

OVER-RELIANCE ON TECHNOLOGY

Relying solely on automated tools may discourage writers from developing their own proofreading and editing skills. It's essential to use these tools as aids rather than substitutes for careful review.

NOT FOOLPROOF FOR PUNCTUATION

Punctuation errors, especially those related to nuanced usage, may not always be accurately detected by spelling and grammar checkers. Writers still need a good understanding of punctuation rules. Some punctuation may also be flagged as incorrect because of writing style.

LIMITED FEEDBACK ON WRITING STYLE

While tools can identify grammatical errors, they may not offer insights into refining one's writing style. Writers looking to improve their overall writing may need additional feedback.

Oftentimes, you'll see spellings that you may think are typos. Most times, this happens when the book is written by an English author instead of an American author. Although both spellings may be correct, you typically will want to stay consistent in your spelling format.

British	American		British	American
-ise, -yse	**-ize, -yze**		**-ae -oe**	**-e**
apologise	apologize		leukaemia	leukemia
organise	organize		encyclopaedia	encyclopedia
recognise	recognize		manoeuvre	maneuver
analyse	analyze		oestrogen	estrogen
breathalyse	breathalyze		mediaeval	medieval
paralyse	paralyze		paediatric	pediatric
-our	**-or**		**-nce**	**-nse**
colour	color		defence	defense
rumour	rumor		licence	license
flavour	flavor		offence	offense
harbour	harbor		pretence	pretense
humour	humor			
labour	labor		**add -l**	**no extra -l**
behaviour	behavior		fuelled	fueled
neighbour	neighbor		travelling	traveling
			traveller	traveler
			cancelled	canceled
-re	**-er**			
litre	liter		**others**	
fibre	fiber		grey	gray
theatre	theater		pyjamas	pajamas
centre	center		tyre	tire
calibre	caliber		ageing	aging
metre	meter			
sombre	somber			

Sometimes, authors may get caught up in hitting a pre-established word count. Even in some writing software, there may be a setting to count how many words you've typed that day for a daily goal. Although this may keep you on track for writing, this type of thinking may lead to wordy novels. Word choice and word economy may lower your overall word count, but it will make your book sound better and more professional.

There are different ways to combat wordy paragraphs.

Many authors will tell you to **cut out adverbs**. Although you may think that adverbs are there to describe an action (which they are!), there are much better ways to describe those actions through vocabulary.

The boy angrily walked away.

The boy stomped away.

Use **word economy**; erase the word that.

She cried when she found out that the dog was ill.

She cried when she found out the dog was ill.

Unclear sentences

The chicken is ready to eat.

Is the animal ready to eat some feed, or is the cooked chicken for dinner ready?

Unvaried sentences

Make sure sentences start differently. Vary the length of your sentences and employ use of complex and compound sentences.

Redundancy

The businessmen collaborated together.

Using the Thesaurus

The thesaurus truly is an extraordinary book for writers. Using creative words become easier when there are a plethora of words to use at your fingertips. Lists of synonyms may seem tedious, but in the end, using words taken from a thesaurus makes your writing exciting and even clearer than before.

She laughed as he fell to the ground.

The sentence above may be very plain. To spruce it up, we may consult the services of the thesaurus.

Laughed: chuckle, giggle, grin, howl, roar, scream, shriek, snicker, snort, whoop

Fell (look up the word fall): collapse, crash, decline, decrease, depreciate, diminish, dip, dive, dwindle, ease, go down, land, plummet, plunge, settle, sink, slip, slump, stumble, tumble

With the words from a thesaurus, you can change a sentence to sound more appealing and give visual context.

She roared with laughter as he plummeted to the ground.

She chuckled as he stumbled to the ground.

Although synonyms are used, the sentences may change ever so slightly. Stumbled and plummeted have somewhat different meanings and visualizations. Roaring with laughter and chuckling are also two different variations of laughing with varying degrees of intensity.

The word "very" is overrated. The best thing you can do is delete very and replace the following word with an impactful word or phrase. This can be done with the help of a thesaurus.

Very happy - jubilant, ecstatic, thrilled, overjoyed

Very valuable - precious, treasured, prized

Very bright - brilliant, radiant, dazzling

Very hungry - ravenous, starved, famished

Very strange - extraordinary, bizarre, remarkable

Very serious - severe, solemn, deliberate

Very funny - hilarious, ludicrous, riot

Very beautiful - exquisite, magnificent, marvelous

Creative Wording

ALLITERATION

The repetition of a beginning sound. Alliterations can create a sing-song effect. This can be done a few times in the novel, but it shouldn't be overdone. Poems will have alliteration more than novel writing.

Her hair was long, luscious, and light.

ALLUSION

Allusions refer to other works, people, or events outside of your own works. For example, calling someone a Jezebel refers to Jezebel from the Bible. Someone may refer to a person as a Scrooge, referring to Sir Arthur Conan Doyle's *A Christmas Carol*. Other popular allusions are Pandora's Box, Draconian Rule, and Romeo and Juliet. The trick to writing a successful allusion is to reference something well-known.

"Well aren't you a modern Sherlock?"

ONOMATOPOEIA

As most school-agers try to figure out how to spell onomatopoeia, the definition itself is hardly complicated. An onomatopoeia is simply the written version of a sound being made. Younger children will learn to say woof, hiss, or meow at an early age, mimicking animals. Other words may include bang, whoosh, and splash. These are common stand-alone words in comics, but sneaking some onomatopoeia in your sentences may provide familiar details regarding sounds for your readers.

The radiator hissed as she slept on the couch.

Bang! The door slammed shut.

PERSONIFICATION

A tactic used by writers such as John Steinbeck to describe nature, personification makes things come alive. New York City is called the city that never sleeps, although it is technically the people who "never sleep". Trees whispering, oceans calling, wind blowing, and toys flying off the shelves during Christmas are all personifications. Personifications are common in poetry and everyday speech.

The new books written by the mystery author started flying off the shelves.

ANALOGY, METAPHOR, SIMILE

A comparison of two things to make a point. Many times, a metaphor or a simile is used. Although very similar, they have their own differences.

An **analogy** is saying something is like something else to make some explanatory point. Analogies can be all shapes and sizes; some can even last a whole short story if written well.

"A good speech should be like a woman's skirt: long enough to cover the subject and short enough to create interest." - Winston S. Churchill

A **metaphor** describes something in terms of something else. We often hear a metaphor without realization because it has become part of our vocabulary. Common metaphors include a blanket of snow, a heart of stone, and time is money. Try to use creative and original metaphors in writing.

The cement was lava that day at the pool.

A **simile**, somewhat similar to a metaphor, uses the words **like** and **as**.

He was as white as a sheet.

A common simile could be rewritten to become a more creative sentence.

He was as white as my notebook pages.

He was as white as this morning's oat milk.

Repetition

Although repetition may sound annoying, it may enunciate a part of your writing when used wisely. Used a lot in poetry, it may be added to your writing for dramatic effect.

An **epistrophe** is when the same word is repeated at the end of every phrase. **Anaphora** is when the same word is repeated at the beginning of every phrase. It is not uncommon to have words repeated randomly. There are even some books where the word is at the beginning and end of a chapter or even an entire book.

"Hatred was spreading everywhere, blood was being spilled everywhere, wars were breaking out everywhere." Shusaku Endo, Deep River

Situation to Action

Highlighting the "Show, Don't Tell" concept, emotions can play a huge role in actions. On the surface, the novel shouldn't tell you what is happening, but rather show you how it's happening.

A good story can have a range of emotions, but a better story will insinuate that the protagonist is angry without using the word angry by showing you their actions and reactions.

The use of adrenaline and basic psychology can go a long way. The most popular being fight, flight, freeze, and fawn. (Fawn is trying to please to avoid any conflict.)

face going pale	isolating	blaming others
panicking	slow movements	clenches fist
jerky movements	lack of motivation	laughs nervously
mind racing	fatigue	squints
survival mode	blushing	doesn't use contractions
short shallow breathing	avoiding eye contact	jumbles words
panicking	changing the conversation	makes mindless mistakes
narrowing eyes	rubbing different parts of their body	plays with hair
heavy breathing	stuttering	call people by the wrong names
lying	slouching	
feeling bad about themselves	getting quiet	stumbles
anxious thoughts	shaking head	chews on fingernails
glaring	backing away	falls asleep in random places
stomping	dismissal	shaking
snapping	justification	picks skin
grinding teeth	fidgeting	irritated at small things
red eyes		yawns

Know how your character process emotions.

What are the things they fear?	Do they anger easily?
Are some of those fears irrational?	Do they get nasty?
How do they think through their options?	Are they petty?
How fast is their reaction time?	Calculating or impulsive?
Do they get defensive?	Do they get anxious easily?

The Five Senses

You may see a plate of food and know the aroma, taste, or texture. Our brain usually can see everyday items around us, and we instantly know what it will feel like. When your brain combines multiple sensory inputs to enhance response, it is called multi-sensory integration.

Vestibular and **proprioception** are connected to the tactile sense (touch) and can be defined as two other senses. The vestibular sense involves movement and balance. Proprioception lets us perceive the location, movement, and action of body parts without using our sight.

Others may argue that the sense of touch can be divided into different types of senses, including heat, pressure, vibrations, and pain.

The famous sixth sense (although not scientific) is a common theme in novels. Usually considered an intuition, extra sensory perception or a sixth sense may help your character in tricky situations.

Visual – sight

Olfactory – smell

Auditory – sounds

Gustatory – taste

Tactile – touch

TIP

The use of metaphors and similes will help describe senses.

Sight

Writing visuals are the most important details in a novel regarding senses. Visualizing the words on the pages is necessary, or the reader will be bored and uninterested, maybe even confused.

Specific and Descriptive Language

Instead of general terms, use specific and descriptive language that paints a clear picture. For example, instead of saying "tree," you might say "towering redwood."

Multi-Sensory Writing

Describe not only what things look like but also how they feel, smell, sound, or even taste.

Show, Don't Tell

Instead of stating facts, show the details through action and sensory perception. Describe the scene through the eyes of your characters. This can also be done by using nostalgia and feelings about particular objects.

Analogies and Metaphors

Analogies and metaphors can create powerful and imaginative visual connections.

Key Details

Highlight key details that paint the whole picture.

Rule of Three

Satisfying, effective, and memorable.

Perspectives

Write from the viewpoint of your character. What details would they notice?

Read

The more you read, the more you will grasp how to describe visuals that are appealing to the reader.

The intricate lacework on the antique doily caught the sunlight, creating delicate shadows that danced across the polished mahogany table.

The artist's brushstrokes on the canvas revealed a world of vivid colors, each stroke contributing to the mesmerizing tapestry of the painting.

The dew-kissed spiderweb glistened in the morning light, a delicate masterpiece woven among the blades of grass.

The old leather-bound book showed signs of wear, with faded gold lettering and dog-eared pages that whispered of countless readings.

The intricate patterns of the Persian rug told stores of craftsmanship, with rich hues and detailed motifs that seemed to come alive.

The stained-glass window bathed the chapel in a kaleidoscope of colors, casting a vibrant mosaic of light on the worn wooden pews.

The ornate wrought-iron gate featured intricate scrollwork, a testament to the skilled hands that had crafted this entrance to a hidden garden.

"The flowers were unnecessary, for two o'clock a greenhouse arrived from Gatsby's, with innumerable receptacles to contain it. An hour later the front door opened nervously, and Gatsby, in a white flannel suit, silver shirt, and gold-colored tie, hurried in. He was pale, and there were dark signs of sleeplessness beneath his eyes."

–F. Scott Fitzgerald, The Great Gatsby

Dark spruce forest frowned on either side the frozen waterway. The trees had been stripped by a recent wind of their white covering of frost, and they seemed to lean towards each other, black and ominous, in the fading light. A vast silence reigned over the land. The land itself was a desolation, lifeless, without movement, so lone and cold that the spirit of it was not even that of sadness. There was a hint in it of laughter, but of a laughter more terrible than any sadness—a laughter that was mirthless as the smile of the sphinx, a laughter cold as the frost and partaking of the grimness of infallibility. It was the masterful and incommunicable wisdom of eternity laughing at the futility of life and the effort of life. It was the Wild, the savage, frozen-hearted Northland Wild.

– Jack London, White Fang

Touch

abrasive	damp	gelatinous	level	sandy	sweaty
bald	dehydrated	glassy	limp	saturated	swollen
barbed	dense	glazed	lined	scalding	syrupy
bendable	dented	glossy	loose	scarred	thick
blemished	dirty	gooey	luke-warm	scraped	tingly
blistered	doughy	grainy	lumpy	scratched	thin
bloated	drenched	granular	malleable	sculptured	thorny
blunt	dry	greasy	metallic	serrated	throbbing
bristly	dusty	grimy	moist	shaggy	tiled
broken	electrified	gritty	mosaic	sharp	tough
bubbly	embossed	grooved	mushy	sheer	unblemished
bulging	enameled	grubby	narrow	silky	unbreakable
bulky	encrusted	hairy	neat	slick	uncomfortable
bumpy	engorged	hard	oily	slimy	uneven
burning	engraved	harsh	ornamented	slippery	uniform
bushy	etched	hollow	padded	smooth	varnished
caked	even	hot	patterned	soaked	velvety
carved	fat	icy	pleated	soapy	vibrating
chapped	feathery	impenetrable	pliable	soft	warm
chunky	filmy	imprinted	plush	soggy	wavy
circular	firm	indented	pointy	soiled	wet
clammy	flat	inflated	polished	solid	wide
clean	fleecy	inlaid	porous	sopping	wiry
coarse	flimsy	inscribed	prickly	spiny	withered
cold	fluffy	ironed	pulpy	spongy	wobbly
cool	fluted	irregular	ragged	springy	woolly
corrugated	fragile	itchy	ribbed	stagnant	woven
cratered	freezing	jagged	ridged	stiff	wrinkly
creamy	frigid	knitted	rigid	sticky	
crocheted	frothy	layered	rough	strong	
cushioned	furry	leafy	rubbery	stubbly	
damaged	fuzzy	leathery	rusty	stucco	

When writing touch, know the difference between sight and touch. While the two may be used synonymously, its always good to know whether the character is touching something as opposed to seeing something and knowing what it feels like.

The soft, velvety petals of the rose brushed against my fingertips as I carefully arranged the bouquet.

Running my hand across the coarse, weathered bark of the ancient oak tree, I felt the history embedded in its textured surface.

The cool, smooth surface of the marble countertop provided a refreshing touch as I prepared dinner in the kitchen.

The fine, powdery sand sifted through my fingers at the beach, leaving a gentle, soothing sensation in its wake.

The warm, fuzzy blanket enveloped me in a cocoon of comfort, its soft fibers a soothing caress against my skin.

In the sentences above, notice that some words, though not describing a sensation of touch, is mentally stimulating. Descriptions like *marble countertop* offer the reader more of an insight to how the countertop feels. *Cocoon of comfort*, gives the reader a feeling of warmth and coziness.

Verbs such as *brushed* and *sifted* also aid in tactile imagery.

Taste

The taste may be difficult to explain because when we describe a flavor, our descriptions generally describe things as either the usual sweet, sour, or bitter, along with the description of food we've eaten before.

Some food products, such as unique chocolates or coffees, will give a few descriptive words for the flavor to distinguish the different types of chocolate or coffee. If there were no other words, such as bold or earthy, the coffee would just be coffee flavor.

The rich aroma of freshly brewed coffee enveloped the room, promising a robust and invigorating flavor with each sip.

As I bit into the warm, flaky croissant, the delicate layers melted on my tongue, releasing a buttery sweetness that lingered.

The zesty salsa danced on my taste buds, with a perfect balance of tangy tomatoes, fiery jalapeños, and fresh cilantro.

The velvety chocolate mousse delighted my palate, its decadent richness leaving a lingering sweetness that was pure indulgence.

Crisp and refreshing, the apple slices provided a juicy crunch, their natural sweetness making for a satisfying and healthy snack.

The aged cheddar cheese exhibited a sharp and nutty profile, its complex flavors unfolding with every savory bite.

The spicy curry dish left a tingling heat on my tongue, a symphony of exotic spices that transported me to distant lands.

The velvety smoothness of the vanilla custard left a trail of sweet nostalgia, reminiscent of childhood desserts and simple joys.

Phrases such as *exotic spices* give you an idea that the taste is something that may be unfamiliar. Verbs such as *melted* and *danced* also give imagination to how it feels to eat such foods.

Taste

acidic	candy-like	fresh	metallic	sour
acrid	chalky	fruity	nutty	spicy
alkaline	chemical	full-bodied	pungent	sulfur
ashy	citrus	green	rancid	sweet
bitter	clean	herbal	rich	tangy
bittersweet	cooling	honeyed	robust	tart
briny	delicate	lactic	savory	woody
burnt	earthy	lipid	sharp	yeasty
buttery	fiery	medicinal	smoky	zesty

Taste can also incorporate tactile senses as food also has texture. Food preparation also plays an important role in knowing what the food tastes or feels like.

Texture

airy	crunchy	flaky	juicy	stale
buttery	crusty	fluffy	paste	sticky
chewy	delicate	gooey	pureed	succulent
chopped	doughy	granulated	silky	tender
creamy	elastic	ground	slimy	velvety
crispy	fine	hearty	smooth	
crumbly	fizzy	jelly	sparkling	

Preparation

baked	caramelized	glazed	rotisserie	steeped
blackened	charred	infused	salted	stewed
blanched	deep-fry	marinated	sauteed	stir-fry
boiled	dehydrated	pickled	seared	whipped
braised	fermented	poached	simmered	
breaded	fried	pressure-cooked	smoked	
broiled	fry	roasted	steamed	

Sounds

Sounds can be split into two groups—the description of sounds and the actual names of sounds or onomatopoeias. Auditory perceptions may also be different depending on the reader, especially onomatopoeias. One person may say bow-wow as another says bark. The same is true for words such as splish and splash, babble and bubble, screech and shriek.

Just like synonyms, some words may have slight differences depending on the situation, such as plop and plunk. One may visualize a plop on a hard surface, while plunk is the same motion but into water.

abrasive	complex	forceful	listenable	pounding	sporadic
aggressive	congested	fragmented	lively	powerful	staccato
airy	constant	frantic	loud	pulsating	static
almighty	continuous	full	lush	punch	steady
ambiance	crescendo	graceful	mellow	pure	structured
articulate	crisp	grainy	melodic	quiet	stylish
atmosphere	dark	grinding	monotonous	rapid	sweet
audible	deafening	growing	mood	rasp	symbolic
balanced	decay	grungy	moving	refined	tasteful
bassy	delicate	harmonic	muffled	regular	temperature
blanketed	dense	haunting	musical	repetitive	tempo
blurred	depth	heavy	mysterious	resonant	tenor
boomy	disharmonic	hollow	nasal	resounding	textured
bouncy	disjointed	honky	natural	rhythmic	thunderous
boxy	distant	howling	nimble	rich	tone
brassy	dull	hushed	noisy	roaring	toneless
breathy	dynamic	hypnotic	nostalgic	rowdy	treble
bright	ear-splitting	impactful	off beat	rush	tumultuous
brilliant	elegant	improvised	ornate	sharp	tuned
broken	erratic	inaudible	overtone	shrill	tuneless
chaotic	euphonic	instrumental	percussive	signature	uncommon
chesty	explosive	intense	periodic	sloppy	unending
clamorous	expressive	invigorating	piercing	slow	uniform
clear	exquisite	irregular	pitch	smeared	unintelligible
coarse	faded	jarring	pleasing	smooth	unpredictable
cohesive	fast	layered	polluted	soft	vocal
colorful	feeling	liquid	polyphonic	soothing	warm

achoo
ahem
arf
argh
baa
babble
bam
bang
barf
bark
bash
bawl
beating
beep
belch
bellow
blab
blare
blast
blaze
bleat
bleep
blimp
bling
blip
blow
blub
blurt
boing
boink
bong
bonk
boo
boo-hoo
boom
boop
bop
bow-wow
bubble

bumble
bump
burble
burp
burst
buzz
cackle
caw
cha-cha
cha-ching
chant
chat
chatter
cheep
chime
chink
chirp
chit-chat
chitty
chomp
choo-choo
chortle
chug
clack
clamor
clang
clangor
clank
clap
clash
clatter
click
clickety-clack
clink
clip clop
clonk
cluck
clunk

cock a doodle doo
coo
cough
crack
crackle
crash
creak
crinkle
croak
crow
crunch
crush
cry
cuckoo
ding
ding dong
ding-a-ling
dong
dribble
drip
drizzle
drone
drum
drumming
echo
explode
fart
fizz
fizzle
flap
flash
flick
fling
flip-flop
flog
flop
flush
flutter

gaggle
gallop
garble
gargle
gasp
gibber
giggle
gloop
glug
gnash
gnaw
gobble
gong
grind
groan
growl
grumble
grunt
gulp
gurgle
gush
hack
haha
hee-haw
hiccup
hiss
holler
honk
hoo
hoot
howl
huff
hum
humph
hush
jab
jabber
jangle
jar

jingle
ka-ching
kaboom
kapow
ker-ching
kerplink
knock
lap
lisp
mash
meow
mew
moan
moo
mumble
munch
murmur
mutter
neigh
nibble
nuzzle
oink
oomph
ooze
pad
paddle
pat
patter
peep
phew
ping
ping pong
pip
pipe
pitter
pitter patter
plink
plop
pluck

plunk
pong
poof
pop
pow
puff
puke
pump
purr
putter
quack
racket
rap
rat-a-tat
rattle
rev
ribbit
ring
rip
ripple
roar
rumble
rush
rustle
scour
scramble
scrape
scratch
scream
screech
scrub
scrunch
scuffle
shatter
shiver
shout
shred
shriek
shudder

shuffle
shush
sigh
sizzle
skip
Slam
slap
slash
slither
slobber
slosh
slurp
slush
smack
smooch
snap
snarl
sneak
sneer
sneeze
snicker
sniff
sniffle
snip
snore
snort
sob
spank
spark
sparkle
spit
splash
splat
splatter
splish
sploosh
splosh
splutter
sprinkle

sputter
squawk
squeak
squeal
squelch
squirt
squish
stamp
stomp
strum
suck
swarm
swat
sway
swell
swish
swoop
swoosh
tap
tapping
tattle
tear
tearing
throb
thrum
thud
thump
thwack
tic-toc
tick
ting
tinkle
tiptoe
tock
toot
trickle
trill
twang
tweet

twinkle
ugh
utter
vroom
wail
whack
wham
wheeze
whimper
whine
whinny
whip
whirl
whirr
whisper
whistle
whizz
whomp
whoop
whoosh
woof
yack
yadda yadda
yap
yell
yelp
yip
yowl
zap
zing
zip
zonk
zoom

Scents

"The smell of a grow room is the scent of transpiration, of fecund exertion. It's the trapped sweat of a high school locker room, the funk of a hockey jersey steaming on a radiator." -Bruce Barcott, Weed the People

acid	earthy	lemony	perfumed	sickly
acrid	evocative	lilac	pine	skunky
airy	faint	lime	plastic	smelly
ambrosial	feminine	loamy	powerful	smoky
antiseptic	fishy	masculine	pungent	sour
aroma	floral	medicinal	putrid	spicy
aromatic	flowery	minty	rancid	spoiled
billowy	fragrance	moist	rank	stale
biting	fragrant	moldy	reek	stench
citrusy	fresh	musky	repulsive	stinking
clean	fruity	musty	rich	stuffy
comforting	funky	nasty	ripe	sweaty
coppery	garlicky	nauseating	rose	sweet
crisp	heady	odor	rotten	tangy
damp	heavy	odorless	savory	tart
delicate	intoxicating	odorous	scent	whiff
delicious	laden	overpowering	scented	wispy
dirty	leathery	peachy	sharp	woody

Other Senses

time	sound direction	empathy
depth	perception	motion
moisture	logical or illogical leaps	location and direction
muscle exhaustion	emotions of objects	kinesthetics
barriers	dirtiness	hunger
relative sizing	pain	fatigue
moisture	awareness of surroundings	heartbeat
balance	awareness of size	temperature
weight	sensations	analyzation

Conflict

Although you should have a good idea of what conflict will be in your story, sometimes you have room to create more conflict to make sure your story stays exciting and the plot doesn't become dry.

A character flaw (or positive) creates a barrier

Drawbacks of using objects

Some characters are two-faced and will betray the protagonist

Drawbacks of using magic

Your character accidentally created more conflict from a decision

Choices have both negatives and positives

Give your protagonist two motives; one has to be sacrificed to achieve the other

The protagonist's past works against them

Your character is sometimes wrong

Fracture friendships and alliances

Create sympathy towards the antagonist

Insert misunderstandings

Unpredictable natural events

Murphy's Law

Magic Creation

Magic is arguably is the most conflict creating situation in a fantasy world, but to avoid plot holes, magic has to be created carefully.

Magic has rules, but the creation of rules is entirely flexible. The rules however, must stay consistent within the book.

What are the drawbacks of magic? Is it mental, physical, or emotional?

Do they need tools such as wands and spells?

How do people learn magic?

Can anyone learn it, or does it come from genetics?

How involved is magic in everyday life?

How long does it take to master magic?

How many different types of magic are there?

Does magic evolve?

How accepted is magic in society?

Are there careers in magic?

Are there any laws against magic?

Is there "good and bad" magic?

Can someone lose their magic?

How would someone lose their magic?

Do emotions affect magic?

Is there specialty magic?

What are the limitations?

What can happen if someone uses the wrong spell?

Writer's block can be a common challenging obstacle. The key is to find strategies that work for you and to approach your writing with a positive and open mindset.

Take breaks

Short breaks can help prevent burnout. Some authors may even take long breaks. Step away from writing and engage in a different activity.

Set realistic goals

Break down your writing tasks into smaller, manageable goals. Setting big goals from the beginning may be discouraging.

Switch writing tools

If you typically write on a computer, try switching to pen and paper or vice versa. Some authors may love the feel and sound of a typewriter and writing in a notebook gives you fewer constraints in regards to time and location as opposed to a computer.

Change your environment

Move to a different space to stimulate your mind. A change of scenery can break the monotony and provide a fresh perspective. A local coffee shop or a library can be a place to find the right ambience for your writing needs.

Freewriting

Set aside a specific amount of time to write without any constraints or expectations. Allow your thoughts to flow freely, even if they are unrelated to your project. This can help loosen up your creativity.

Physical movement

Taking a walk or doing some exercises can help stimulate your mind.

Write out of order

If you're stuck on a particular chapter, skip it and work on a different chapter. When writing subplots, this can come in handy. You can always go back and connect the pieces later.

Read

Immerse yourself in related literature or conduct additional research on your topic. Reading may spark fresh ideas or inspiration.

Discuss your ideas

Share your thoughts and ideas with a friend, writing group, or mentor. They may have some fresh ideas to help overcome a writers block.

Set a routine

Establish a consistent writing routine. Train yourself to work and concentrate during that time.

Seek inspiration

Engage in activities that inspire you, whether it's reading a favorite book, listening to music, or exploring nature.

Practice mindfulness or meditation

Clear your mind through mindfulness or meditation techniques. Relaxing your mind can help alleviate stress and open the mental pathways for creativity.

Eat healthy

Easing snacks and unhealthy foods is an easy habit to get into when sitting and writing. Opt for less sugar and invest in some bite-sized vegetable snacks. Avoid sugary drinks.

Polishing the Plot

When writing your plot and even when writing your novel, several questions should be asked. Some of these questions can't be answered until you've spent a considerable amount of time on the book, but they are good guidelines to help you keep your novel interesting.

Does the story border reality or is realistic enough to be believable?

What's at stake?

Is the setting easy to pick up on?

Does the story have enough scenery?

Is it a fair fight?

Is there a uniqueness to the plot?

Do you care about the elements?

Is it too personal?

Like Water for Chocolate is divided into 12 chapters, one for each month of the year. On top of that, each chapter comes with a Mexican recipe that aligns with an event in the main character's life. The television series *24*, is split into 24 episodes, each episode being an hour long in real-time. Think about any cool ways to make your novel stand out.

THE FOUR C'S

Clarity: Are the points clear? Is there focus in your sentences and situations?

Consistency: Is the style consistent? Are characters consistent in the way they talk and act?

Conciseness: Do you have all the best wording possible?

Completeness: Does the whole story make sense? Are there any parts left out of the story?

Alerian Academy

What Authors Say

"When I hear the hypercritical quarreling about grammar and style, the position of the particles, etc., etc., stretching or contracting every speaker to certain rules of theirs. I see that they forget that the first requisite and rule is that expression shall be vital and natural, as much as the voice of a brute or an interjection: first of all, mother tongue; and last of all, artificial or father tongue. Essentially your truest poetic sentence is as free and lawless as a lamb's bleat."

Henry David Thoreau

"Substitute 'damn' every time you're inclined to write 'very;' your editor will delete it and the writing will be just as it should be."

Mark Twain

"Grammar is a piano I play by ear."

Joan Didion

"The road to hell is paved with adverbs."

Stephen King

"If it can be cut out, then CUT IT OUT. Everything non-essential that you can eliminate strengthens what's left."

Alexander Mackendrick

"Let me live, love, and say it well in good sentences."

Sylvia Plath

"When I wrote Beloved, I thought about it for three years. I started writing the manuscript after thinking about it, and getting to know the people and getting over the fear of entering that arena, and it took me three more years to write it. But those other three years I was still at work, though I hadn't put a word down."

Toni Morrison

The first draft of anything is shit. "
Ernest Hemingway

There are three difficulties in authorship;
to write any thing worth the publishing
— to find honest men to publish it — and
to get sensible men to read it.

Charles Caleb Colton

Publishing

Pen Names

If you haven't already, establish if you want to use your real name or a pen name. Some writers are famous for using pen names, while others use them for various reasons.

J.K. Rowling, Robert Galbraith

Real name: Joanne Rowling

JK Rowling used an initial of K to make her gender unknown. K isn't even a middle initial. She published the book Robert Galbraith after becoming a well-known author.

Richard Bachman

Real name: Stephen King

Like Robert Galbraith, Richard Bachman was created after Stephen King was a well-known and respected author. Stephen King wrote under Bachman's name to not saturate the market with his own name. He also released it without marketing so that he could experiment with talent and luck as an author.

Clive Hamilton and N. W. Clerk

Real name: C. S. Lewis

The well-known author had two different pen names, Clive Hamilton for poems and N.W. Clerk as a book about bereavement after the death of his wife. Both were made to protect his reputation at Oxford University.

Mary Westmacott

Real name: Agatha Christie

Agatha Christie, the Queen of Crime, was already a successful writer and created Mary Westmacott, who wrote six novels that were not her usual style. The pen name was a secret for almost 20 years.

Currer Bell

Real name: Charlotte Brontë

The Brontë sisters, Charlotte, Emily, and Anne, were all encouraged to change their names for their literary works. Back then, it wasn't uncommon for women to experience prejudice from publishers and readers. Although writing under pen names, the secret was hardly a secret.

George Orwell

Real name: Eric Arthur Blair

Lewis Carroll

Real name: Charles Lutwidge Dodgson

Mark Twain

Real name: Samuel Langhorne Clemens

Publish-ready

EDIT - There is nothing worse than a manuscript riddled with mistakes and unresolved stories that you may think are "ready-to-go".

Make sure your title is captivating and inciting. Your book title should be unique and easy to remember.

Spend some energy on finding professional editing and proofreading services. Some editors are costly and charge by the hour.

Some writing programs are able to format your book so it's print-ready.

Although not professional, finding volunteer readers can be easily done online in book forums for overall impressions and unbiased reviews.

Design and formatting must satisfy the reader and the printers. Familiarize yourself with margins, trim sizes, layouts, and gutters.

You may want to hire a graphic designer to create a cover. Design a book cover that draws in readers. Not only is the cover a first impression, but it is also a glimpse into what genre or style it is. A thriller or mystery would have a dark cover, while chick-lit may be light and airy.

Write a great book description for the back cover. One of the first things a potential reader will do is pick up the book and look at the summary. If the summary doesn't intrigue the reader, they'll return it to the shelf.

Decide if you want to create an audiobook as well.

The first step for publishing is to decide which route is right for you

- **Literary agent**

- **Publishing company**

- **Self-Publishing**

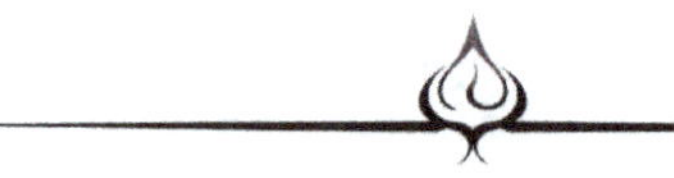

Alerian Academy

Sending your work to a publishing company typically involves submitting a query letter, book proposal, and a manuscript.

Research publishers

Not all publishers are the same. Some play to a more specific genre or style. They also have different reputations. Beware of small unknown companies as there are also scam publishers.

Check submission guidelines

Each publisher has submission guidelines. They provide specific details on how to submit your work for review.

Manuscript

make sure your manuscript is perfect and in condition to be printed. Refer back to the publisher guidelines on formatting rules.

Write a query letter or book proposal

Similar to a cover letter, send in your query letter that introduces yourself. Sometimes, you may send in a book proposal as well that is similar to a business plan.

Bonus

Include a self-addressed stamped envelope

Keep track of submissions

Follow-up

Be patient

Handle rejections well

Some new authors who want to publish their books usually will find a literary agent. A literary agent will take care of the busy work of convincing publishers to publish your book, after you convince the literary agent that it is really worth publishing first.

Getting a literary agent may be difficult. They are busy people receiving hundreds of letters. Literary agents are not people you hire but people who choose the authors to work with. Like finding a job, finding a literary agent who will work with you may require a dozen "applications" before even receiving a response.

Research literary agents who represent the types of books that you are offering. There are resources online that can help you find agents. Sometimes, you may get lucky by having a mutual friend or meeting them at a writing conference.

Many times, agents will have submission guidelines. Draft a compelling query letter introducing yourself, providing a brief synopsis of your book, and highlighting why you believe the agent is a good fit. Submit letters to multiple agents and tailor each query to the specific agent.

A literary agent serves as an author's guide, advocate, and business partner, helping them navigate the publishing landscape and succeed in their writing careers. The specific tasks may vary depending on the agent's focus, the genre they represent, and their approach to the industry.

Imagine a literary agent as a lawyer for your writing. It is in their best interests for you to succeed.

Representation

Literary agents represent authors and their literary works.

Negotiation

Agents negotiate contracts with publishers on behalf of their clients. This includes securing favorable advances, royalties, and other contractual details.

Submission of manuscripts

Agents submit manuscripts to publishers to secure a publishing deal.

Market knowledge

Agents stay informed about market trends, genre preferences, and publishing industry changes.

Alerian Academy

Editorial feedback

Agents provide editorial feedback to their clients to improve the marketability and quality of their manuscripts before submission to publishers.

Career guidance

Agents offer career guidance and advice to authors, helping them navigate the complexities of the publishing industry.

Career guidance

Agents act as advocates for their clients, ensuring that their interests are protected and that they receive fair compensation for their work.

Contract review

Agents review publishing contracts to ensure that the terms are fair and in the best interest of their clients. They may negotiate changes to the contract with the publisher.

Royalty Management

Agents monitor and manage royalty payments to ensure that authors receive accurate and timely compensation for their published works.

Marketing and Promotion

While publishers handle much of the marketing, agents may play a role in helping to strategize and promote their clients' works, especially in collaboration with the publisher's marketing efforts.

Industry Networking

Agents build and maintain relationships with editors, publishers, and other industry professionals. Networking is crucial for staying informed about industry trends and opportunities.

Legal knowledge

Agents should have a good understanding of publishing contracts and relevant legal issues to protect their clients' rights and interests.

Client Support

Agents provide emotional support and encouragement to their clients throughout the often challenging process of writing, submitting, and publishing a book.

Self-Publishing

Self-Publishing puts all the control in your hands. This is the option to take if you want to create and sell your book from start to finish. Unlike publishers and literary agents, you'll most likely have to start from scratch. Marketing the book will have to become a priority as authors without agents will not have the connections to make the book successful right away.

Find a platform

There are several platforms for you to publish your book. Each one is unique in price, promotion, royalties, and options so its always a good idea to find out which one suits your needs best.

Purchase an ISBN (International Standard Book Number)

Research to see if you need to purchase an ISBN. Some platforms provide free ISBNs, but some will require you to buy your own. The ISBN will be permanently connected to your book and is a requirement to print and sell in most stores.

Set a price

Determine the price for your e-book or print book. Analyze market trends with similar books. Consider running promotional campaigns or discounts, especially when launching.

Market your book

Develop a marketing plan. Identify categories and keywords to help readers find your book. Get book reviews. This can be done through peer groups or even forums. Find friends and family that will help you promote your book. Use third-party promotional services.

Create an author platform

Build an online presence. This can include a website, social media profiles, a blog, and a mailing list to connect with your readers.

Print Options

Figure out which printing option you want to opt into.

Print-on-demand: Some companies provide POD services where books are only printed when someone orders one. This is an attractive option for those who don't know how many books will sell. It's often hard to know what the POD quality will look like, as the book doesn't physically pass your hands before reaching the customer.

E-book: With modern technology, e-books are easily made and distributed. E-books can be uploaded and bought instantly, and there are no printing fees attached. Most e-book platforms will streamline the process by giving you fields to fill out for your book to make sure it is placed correctly in the genre and sub-genre of the book selling platform.

Self-printing: Ordering a bulk amount of books can be more profitable than POD for you in the long run. You can sell the books yourself. This is a time-consuming option but may end up being more rewarding. With self-printing, you know what the quality is, but you are in charge of distribution, which may be a hassle.

Distribution

Depending on your selected printing options, analyze how you will market and handle the distribution of books.

Legalities and copyright

Ensure you have copyright protection for your work.

Research and Network

Stay informed about the publishing industry, marketing strategies, and new tools. Attend workshops and network with people in the book market. Organize book signings and events. Look for opportunities to get the word around. Use social media to promote your book and keep in touch with potential and existing customers.

Getting it Out

Enter a Literary Contest

The easiest way to get your book noticed is by entering a literary contest. There are only a few reputable contest where you can win a publishing contract or attract a literary agent.

Find a list of all legitimate contests. They may require an entrance fee and it may be genre specific. Each contest has its guidelines and deadlines to get your manuscript submitted.

After you self-publish, you need to promote your work. There are several ways to promote a novel.

Figure out your target audience.

Use keywords for searches.

Set up an engaging website and blog.

Make your own online store.

Send releases to your local newspaper and magazines.

Use social media.

Look for book marketing platforms.

Find places to speak about your book.

Make business cards or other promotional products.

Contact local TV or radio.

Organize readings or book signings at local libraries and bookstores.

Find someone well-known to write a review or promote your book.

Tell everyone you know and ask them to help support you.

Create book samples to hand out.

Make your book available in different formats.

Use book giveaways.

The average author or novelist makes an average of $49,000 per year from writing books. Of course, the amount of money fluctuates depending on how many books they sell.

Other factors, including royalties off of merchandise, also can vary. Authors can also make money from public engagements and teaching.

Most authors will receive an advance with the amount depending on the publishing company. After the advance, they will start making royalties depending on the amount of books being sold, which can range from 5-15%. This can be a dollar to a few dollars per book sold. E-books generally have higher royalties because of the lack of printing fees involved.

Usually, authors will find more success from traditional publishing than self-publishing because publishers have a better network and market. Getting publicity, printing, distribution, and overall marketing is in the hands of professionals when going with traditional publishing.

J. K. Rowling : $1 billion

James Patterson : $800 million

Danielle Steele : $600 million

Stephen King : $500 million

John Grisham : $400 million

JK Rowling makes money off of books, movies, merchandise, and even from Universal Studios theme park.

There are at least 60 movies that are based off of Stephen King books.

Danielle Steele has written more than 190 books.

*Figures are 2023 estimates

Book Facts

Between 500,000 and 1 million books are published yearly, excluding self-published books. Counting self-published and commercially published, over 4 million new books were published in 2022.

A publishing house will often receive more than 5,000 unrequested manuscript submissions annually.

In 2022, more than 12.25 million ebooks were published on Kindle.

As of 2020, a study found 629 of the 1,000 best-selling fiction titles had female authors.

The average American reads 12 books per year.

2.3 million new books were self-published in the U.S. in 2021

The U.S. book industry made over $28 billion in revenue in 2022

Romance is the most popular genre of books sold in the US.

Bookstores are decreasing due to the availability of books online.

Online book sales account for over 70% of all book sales in the US.

The odds of an author getting their work published is between 1% and 2%.

Overcome Obstacles

Twilight was rejected by 14 literary agents.

Life of Pi was rejected by a number of London publishers before its publication in Canada.

Harry Potter and the Philosopher's Stone was rejected more than 10 times by different publishing houses.

Chicken Soup for the Soul had 144 rejections.

Carrie received 30 rejections from publishers.

The Help received 60 rejections from agents for more than three years.

Dune was submitted to 20 publishers before being published by an automotive manual publisher.

A Wrinkle in Time had more than 25 rejections.

Catch-22 was rejected 22 times.

The Diary of Anne Frank: 15 rejections

Lord of the Flies was rejected 20 times.

And to Think That I Saw It on Mulberry Street was rejected by at least 20 publishers.

Gone with the Wind was turned down by almost 40 publishers.

The Wonderful Wizard of Oz was rejected so many times that Frank Baum kept the rejections and recorded them in "A Record of Failure".

Jack London had been rejected 664 times.

Notice that the authors on this list are some of the most well-known authors. Many of these books have become classics and are some of the most well-known and critically acclaimed.

What Authors Say

"Let the reader find that he cannot afford to omit any line of your writing because you have omitted every word that he can spare."

Ralph Waldo Emerson

"The publishing world is very timid. Readers are much braver."

Kiran Desai

"I love deadlines. I like the whooshing sound they make as they fly by."

Douglas Adams

"Publishing a book is like stuffing a note into a bottle and hurling it into the sea. Some bottles drown, some come safe to land, where the notes are read and then possibly cherished, or else misinterpreted, or else understood all too well by those who hate the message. You never know who your readers might be."

Margaret Atwood

"I finished my first book seventy-six years ago. I offered it to every publisher on the English-speaking earth I had ever heard of. Their refusals were unanimous: and it did not get into print until, fifty years later; publishers would publish anything that had my name on it."

George Bernard Shaw

"A writer should say to himself, not 'How can I get more money?' but 'How can I reach more readers without lowering standards?'"

Brian Aldiss

"In matters of truth the fact that you don't want to publish something is, nine times out of ten, a proof that you ought to publish it."

G.K Chesterton

"Work like hell! I had 122 rejection slips before I sold a story."

F. Scott Fitzgerald

Why do I talk about the benefits of failure? Simply because failure meant a stripping away of the inessential. I stopped pretending to myself that I was anything other than what I was, and began to direct all my energy into finishing the only work that mattered to me."

 J.K. Rowling

"If my doctor told me I had only 6 months to live, I'd type a little faster."

Isaac Asimov

When I sit down to write a book, I do not say to myself, 'I am going to produce a work of art.' I write it because there is some lie that I want to expose, some fact to which I want to draw attention, and my initial concern is to get a hearing.

George Orwell

"Best advice on writing I've ever received. Finish."

Peter Mayle

"I went for years not finishing anything. Because, of course, when you finish something, you can be judged. I had pieces that were re-written so many times I suspect it was just a way of avoiding sending them out."

Erica Jong

"When you speak, your words echo across the room. When you write, your words echo across the ages."

Bud Gardner

"Any man who keeps working is not a failure. He may not be a great writer, but if he applies the old-fashioned virtues of hard, constant labor, he'll eventually make some kind of career for himself as writer."

Ray Bradbury

www.ingramcontent.com/pod-product-compliance
Lightning Source LLC
Chambersburg PA
CBHW060159120726
48004CB00007B/1614